D0269149

COWSLIPS AND CLOVER

Also by Elizabeth Cragoe

BUTTERCUPS AND DAISY

COWSLIPS
AND CLOVER

ELIZABETH CRAGOE

HAMISH HAMILTON
LONDON

First published in Great Britain 1977
by Hamish Hamilton Ltd
90 Great Russell Street London

Copyright © 1977 by Elizabeth Cragoe

ISBN 0 241 89761 0

Printed in Great Britain by
Western Printing Services Ltd
Bristol

Prelude

Throughout the long, hot summer, the cattle had worn dusty paths through the parching grass, leading up to the drinking trough at the bottom of the field. When we came into the field to turn on the tap and fill the trough, the thirsty ones would see us, and come galloping up, their hooves raising fine clouds of dust which hung, ghostlike, for minutes after they had passed in the still, hot air.

But it was autumn now. The rain had come, and the fields were green again, except when the heavy dew of a clear morning turned them silver—silver as the filigree of the spiders' webs in the hedgerows, or the trunks of the young ashtrees whose leaves, dropping lightly, lay below them, in a circle on the ground.

There was less need of water now. The cattle took in a lot of moisture with the lush, soaking grass, and one fill of the tank would last them two days where three had not been enough for twenty-four hours in the summer heat. But still the habit lingered, and, when they saw us going to turn on the tap, a few of them would hasten up along their paths, muddy now, and dip their noses in to drink as if they had been waiting for it, in spite of the fact that the trough was half-full already.

The bull was one of these social drinkers, and we admired his size, and the condition that was on him from the good grazing as he buried his face in the tank and noisily sucked up the fresh, splashing water. He was a noble creature. Beautifully bred and well-reared in one of the best herds of Welsh Blacks in the country, he had come to us as a yearling, and now, at three and a half years old, was approaching his full stature. His thick, straight horns sprang from a broad skull thickly covered with shining, black curls. The same short, curly fur extended back

1

over his neck and covered his shoulders, and the massive hump on his withers. His sides and hindquarters were sleek and shiny, for it was not yet time for the long winter coat to show; yet out of this proud, masculine creature's face gazed a pair of the mildest eyes, of deep, lucent brown. He turned these eyes on us now, as he raised his muzzle from the water, and regarded us calmly. I thought his face looked curious, somehow—naked.

'Desmond,' I said, 'Pedwar's got rid of his nose-ring somehow. We'll have to get another one put in.'

'All right, fine,' said Bill, the vet, on the telephone later that afternoon. 'We'll get a new ring for the bull's nose, and we'll do those other jobs you've been talking about at the same time—castrating the young bulls, and a pregnancy diagnosis on the adult females. See you Tuesday afternoon, about 2—both of us.'

'Both of you—why two?'

'One to keep clean for the castrating, the other to get dirty with the P.D.'s. Have them in ready, won't you? See you!'

So on Tuesday we were up early, and out to work without lingering for a second cup of tea. There was a great deal to do. As well as the daily routine work with the hens, which takes up several hours, we had to devise a system of pens and races that would enable us to catch and handle our forty-odd Welsh Black cattle without too much trouble—and some of them can be very recalcitrant indeed!

For two hours we dragged gates around and manoeuvred barricades into gaps before we achieved a design that seemed to satisfy all the job's requirements. The main herd of cattle was to be in the covered yard, from which small puckles of beasts could be driven into a holding pen. The only way out from there was through the cattle crush, in which one beast at a time could be confined and immobilised for the vets to do to it whatever the situation required.

Since we changed over to keeping a suckler herd of Welsh Blacks three years ago instead of the milking Friesians we had had for years, we had lost the close touch with our cattle we had been used to. Dairy cows are tame. Twice a day, for five-sixths of the year, they are used to your hands about them—tying them up, washing the udder, forestripping, putting the

2

milking machine on, and so forth. They are not pets, of course; most cows will move away if you go right up to them in the field. But they are not really afraid of you, and sometimes they quite enjoy a stroke or a pat, or a scratch behind the ears, in passing. But suckler cows are different. You see them every day, but you virtually never touch them; they live, unmolested, guarding their own calves, a very natural life, and are quite unaccustomed to close confinement or the indignity of sub-mitting to the ministrations of human hands.

We get our cattle up about twice a year for a big handling session, when the vet comes in to castrate the young males, and we try to arrange it that any jobs that need doing are worked in at the same time. Each time we have to re-make our handling facilities, and for these strong, half-wild creatures, they have to be solidly put together.

By five to two we were ready, with the cattle in the yard, and all the towels, soap, and buckets of hot water available that the heart of a vet could wish for. At two precisely the senior partner swung into the yard

'Oh what can ail thee, knight-at-arms, alone and palely loitering?' I asked him. 'I thought there were going to be two of you?'

'Oliver's on his way,' he replied

'To play Nervo to your Knox?'

'Nux to my Vomica!'

This promising exchange was cut short by the arrival of Oliver himself, so we repaired to the cattle-yard, and drove the first batch of beasts into the collecting pen.

As luck would have it, the bull came out with the first batch, but nothing any of us could do would persuade him to go into the crush. Several times he tiptoed up to it, extended his big nose, and smelled it; but neither sharp blows nor soft words could persuade him to enter, and before long he began to show signs of getting upset.

'Put him back in with his wives,' said Bill, at last. 'We'll have to tranquillise him.'

So we pushed him back into the big building with the mob, and there the four of us stalked him for five minutes or more until we could get him at a suitable disadvantage for the

3

administration of the tranquilliser. The idea was to get him in a corner with a single layer of cows all around him, over which Bill could lean to give the injection. It didn't take long. One chance, and the needle was in his rump in the blink of an eye. An angry adder has nothing on an experienced vet when it comes to speed of striking.

'How long will it be now before he gets tranquil?'

'All being well, he'll be on the floor before we've finished this lot.'

It was even quicker than that, although the work went quickly. Beast after beast was forced into the crush. Oliver swung the lever that catches the animal's head in a yoke; then he seized its ear, and read out the identifying number. Desmond painted a cross-coded number on the neck, high up, where it could not be licked off, and Bill plunged an experienced arm into the rectum, and told us the approximate age of the foetus he could feel through the bowel and uterine walls.

'Eight months! Surely eight, maybe and-a-half—yes, that's a foot I can feel there!'

I sat on the tractor, and wrote it all down in a notebook, for future reference.

Heifer calves were the lucky ones that day—they passed through the crush unmolested. Adult females were all given the rectal examination for pregnancy—but the young bulls suffered the worst indignity of all. One by one Oliver unmanned them, and the pile of enormous testicles on the ground grew and grew beside him. 'We'll check by these how many I've cut at the end,' he said. 'Remembering, of course, that there was that individual with only one. As long as we don't get another like that!' Curiously enough, the operation seemed to cause hardly any pain, and although the young bulls struggled a little in the crush, not one of them uttered the least bit of a bellow.

There was a total absence of bellowing from another quarter too; and when we went in to bring our second lot of victims from the covered yard, we saw why. Pedwar was lying down, a dazed look on his face, and of a tranquillity that would have delighted the makers of the drug that was now coursing through his veins.

4

'Shall we do him now?'

'No, let's finish this lot first, then I can wash some of the muck off my hands. . . . '

So we continued with our tasks—slicing, painting, groping, or writing, as the case might be.

'Twelve weeks!' 'Number 19.' 'J8330/304!' I wrote it all down. Sometimes Bill would find a cow whose uterus was empty. 'Running with the bull!' he would say, 'That's what they say about this kind in farm sales, don't they? Running with the bull! But he'll get her in calf soon, I've no doubt.'

At last the final matron had shouldered her way out of the crush, and the last testicle bounced onto the concrete. Only the bull remained. How thankful we were for the invention of tranquillising drugs when we went in and found him still lying there heavily, unfocused eyes staring at nothing. He made no response when Oliver haltered him, and pulled the rope tight round his massive horns, and the glossy black curls of his poll. But when Bill produced the new copper ring from his pocket and began to work the pointed end through the hole in his nose, some sensation did begin to filter into his dulled brain. Lurching like a drunkard, he stumbled to his feet, and tried vaguely to shake his massive head. But it was too late now, Oliver had wound the halter rope round a post already, and there was nothing he could do but submit. It was a curious feeling to be able to dominate so easily an animal that could, without much difficulty, have killed us all in a few moments, given the proper use of his faculties.

It does not take long to re-ring a bull once you can hold its head still, and in a minute or two the ends of the ring were screwed together, and the job completed. 'Better push him out into the field while he's on his feet,' said Bill. 'He can sleep it off out there.' So we conducted our Pedwar, reeling majestically, back to the sympathetic bosom of his family.

'Well, that went well enough,' remarked Bill as we all walked up to the yard again. 'Yes,' I said, and 'Very well,' said Desmond. But Oliver cried 'Aaah!' in a great voice, compounded of rage, disgust and despair, and following his pointing finger we all saw the dog, rushing away with a guilty look on its face and something large and pink in its mouth. 'How am

I going to know how many I cut now?' he demanded bitterly. 'That damned dog's pinching my testicles!'

The light was fading as we came into the kitchen, kicked off our boots and set the kettle on to boil. The day's work was done. Our animals—smarting, perhaps, here and there—were back in the peaceful seclusion of their own fields, and apart from the final check round before bed-time, we could consider ourselves finished.

It had been a good day, and we had both enjoyed it—the comradeship, the fun, and the sense of a good job well done. But days like that came more rarely now, when fewer and fewer people worked on each farm, and more and more of the work was done by machines. Farming as a way of life had changed.

Yes, I thought, as I stirred the steaming cup of tea on the table in front of me, it had changed a good deal, even during my lifetime. I was born in 1930, and the horse was still king on the small livestock farms which have always epitomised the pleasure of farming to me. Horses and people—there were plenty of them on every farm in 1935, the year when I first knew I wanted to be a farmer. That was the first year we went to Penhallow, a lovely remote farm in Wales where the sea came up to the very feet of the fields, where everybody was kind, and the sun shone golden every day. We went back every year after that, for a month, re-living the idyll until the war disrupted everything. It was hard to realise that forty years had passed since those days, so distant, and so very bright . . .

There was another lovely farm in Wales too that would always have a place in my memory. Bryn Farm was its proper name, but everybody always referred to it as 'The Bryn'. 'I see they've started cutting the oats down The Bryn,' they'd say, or 'Lovely young gelding Will The Bryn brought back from Bala Sale yesterday!' For it was horses here, too—horses and hand-work. It was in 1943 that I got to know this farm, on the very brink of the tractor explosion that was to transform agriculture before our very eyes.

And by the time I became a farm pupil at Rook's Moat in Shropshire in 1947, the change was irrevocable. Power was all.

6

It is true that labour was still cheap, and there were men in plenty employed to hoe the root-crops and lay the hedges, but the writing was on the wall. Mechanisation was gaining, and the old style of farming with its good-humoured companion-ship, its fun and jokes drawing the sting from the hard work, was becoming more and more a thing of the past.

In our own farm, the process was complete. Changing econo-mics meant that we now farmed without the help of the boy and girl we had employed in our early farming days; routine chores were done by the two of us, and contractors were im-ported to cope with major jobs like making hay or silage. Every-where electric motors took the grind out of work, and the jolly hum of people working together was replaced by the solitary chatter of the internal combustion engine. Even the hens that used to squawk and cackle in the farmyards of my childhood were now confined, the steady hum of the battery shed's forced ventilation taking the place of their lively farmyard voices. It was all changed.

But was it better now? By what standpoint should one judge it? More food was produced by fewer people now, but was that the only criterion? What about the pleasure in the life, the 'job satisfaction' that industrial psychologists love to pontificate about. What had happened to that? Was it illusion—a number-ing of only the sunny hours—that seemed to bathe time past in such a rosy glow? Or had something really gone out of the window when 'farming' changed to 'agriculture'? I remem-bered the words of a friend, now retired, who had started his farming life soon after the war. 'Everybody says it's all much easier now, with all the mechanisation,' he said, 'and in some ways I suppose it is. But although you have machines to help you, you have to look after so many more animals to make a living now. When I started I had ten cows and no machines—I did everything by hand. I milked by hand, I shovelled the muck by hand, I forked it over the fields by hand, and so on. And I made a living. Now I do everything by machine—but I have to keep fifty cows to make the same kind of living. And I reckon I do just as much work driving out the muck from fifty cows with a spreader and a fore-end loader as I did driving it out from ten cows with a hand-fork and a horse and cart.

I'm just as tired at the end of the day, that's for sure—and there are all those machines to go wrong now, too!'

Pouring a second cup of tea, I looked back, as through a long tunnel, on those so-distant days at Penhallow. I tried to purge my memory of sentiment, to see things as they really were. It seemed so long ago that I had walked with dew-soaked shoes, across the paddock to milk Priscilla, or sat on an upturned box in the open-fronted cartshed, learning how to pluck a fowl—so long ago, and so bright . . .

PART I

PENHALLOW

It was always evening when we arrived at Penhallow, and the westering sun turned the encircling sea to a sheet of rippling brass. Memory blends those arrivals, so like one another over the years—the winding, bramble-hung lanes—the car bumping across the fields—the gates to be opened—the first glimpses of the sea. At last, the brilliant green grass of the paddock, with Mr. and Mrs. Evans and Gladys all waiting there, full of smiles, to greet us, while Marion, beaming but shy, hovered in the background.

We would struggle out of the car, cramped after the long drive, feeling the evening breeze cool on the the backs of our crumpled legs. 'Can we go down to the sea?' was always the first question, when all the hellos had been said. Nurse and our mother exchanged glances—and nods. 'Yes, you can,' Nurse would confirm. 'But just down and back, mind. You've had a long day.'

So, leaving the grown-ups to unload the luggage, we scampered up to the top of the paddock. There was a gate, always open, and a low-roofed shed with a pen, where Rupert the boar lived. We always had to sing, as we sidled past him, a little propitiatory song that went 'We're ashamed of Rupert! we're ashamed of Rupert!' but, once through, we were free. The plushy sward of the paddock gave way to a thinner turf, banded with bracken, where the sand showed through—and then there were only fifty yards of wind-sculpted, marram-crested dunes between us and the long, bare, strand of the beach. How the golden light reflected off the dancing sea! How entrancing were the rocks, with weed like emerald-green hair all combed one way by the retreating tide! Sandals were pulled off forthwith and for a few minutes we ran and shouted, alone on the

9

wave-ridged sand, where our footprints fell instantly into round, deliquescent puddles behind us.

But Nurse was not to be trifled with, and soon we had to tear ourselves away. We lagged a little on the way back through the dunes to pick up a pocket full of snail shells, yellow, rosy, or tenderest green, all marvellously freaked and striped in chocolate; but we were not too unwilling to go back, for going to bed in Penhallow was a treat in itself—and besides, did not a whole month lie ahead of us? A stretch of time as long as life itself to children.

Even the most humdrum of daily operations was excitingly different at Penhallow. The bedrooms were floored with linoleum, with flat, oval rush mats on them, and little drifts of sand had a way of coming in at the window, or in people's sandals, and piling up in the corners. You washed in a china basin, in cool soft water that Nurse poured for you from a big jug; and then you poured the dirty water away into an enamel slop-bucket with a lid, and a raffia-bound handle. Water for cleaning teeth, from a different tap in the yard, was in a cut-glass carafe, and you took turns with the glass—Gillian, the eldest, first, Richard next, and me last, as befitted the youngest.

If you needed to go to the lavatory after dark, the final convenience in our bedroom was a handsome commode which spread its welcoming arms in the recess by the window!

'Amenities', in the sense the word is used now, there were none. But who wanted amenities? The very lack of them—the rural simplicity that it connoted—was an amenity in itself. And Nurse's behaviour was another amenity, she held the reins so lightly. At home it would have been unthinkable to eat anything after cleaning our teeth; but, at Penhallow, Gladys used to bring us up biscuits and glasses of a special lemonade, made from crystals—and we were allowed to consume them *in bed!*

It was heaven to be back each year, and as we lay in the dark, smelling the hot wax of the freshly-extinguished candle, we could hear the sea sighing on the beach as the incoming tide rolled up to the foot of the dunes. The beds were higher than our beds at home, and for the first night or two we would fall out with such monotonous regularity that Nurse took to building a barricade of bedroom chairs to keep us within bounds until we had got used to it. But even falling out of bed was all right, because it was Penhallow.

You left watches and clocks behind you when you stepped into the magic world of Penhallow, so I had no idea what time it was as I slipped out of bed in the morning, and dragged on my shirt, shorts, and sandals. It was early; you could tell that. Nobody else was stirring in the house, and when I crept downstairs and pulled open the big front door—never locked—the sun was just rising over the heathery shoulder of Brecyn Hill. The paddock, outside the garden wall, lay deserted, and grey with dew. The geese that kept it plushy as a lawn were still shut up in their house. So were the turkeys, the busy, dung-heap-scratching chickens and the ducks. A curled feather floated lightly on the duckpond in the morning breeze.

I walked round to the back of the house, leaving a trail of big black foot-marks in the dew. The cats were there, waiting, composed and friendly, on the low wall that bounded the cobbled path outside the back door. There was black Happy, who had lost a leg in a trap, and who miaowed dolorously nearly all the time; shrewish, brindled Ginger, with pale-green eyes in a wicked black face; and Ginger's two kittens, Boots and Mup, a pair of beautiful little tortoise-shells. I picked up a hen's feather, and played with Mup for a few minutes, in and out of the stacked driftwood and the green glass floats that somebody had brought up from the beach. She made a long arm to claw the feather out of my hand, then, suddenly changing her mind, sat down with her back to me, and vigorously washed her tummy.

We were all waiting for the same thing, the cats and I. Sooner or later the back door would open, Mrs. Evans would come out, and the new day could then consider itself, officially, to have begun. I loved Mrs. Evans, and to go round with her as she did her morning chores was the height of bliss to me. I liked her soft voice, with its musical Gower intonation—her gentle friendly hazel eyes—and her fresh, tanned, healthy-looking country skin. She was small with black hair looped up in a bun, and she wore an old coat that smelled of cows, and horses, and meal. She never uttered a rebuke, or an impatient word, at least not to me, though she was stricter with Marion, her own daughter. I found her a delightful person to be with.

11

The first job in the morning was milking the cows and, as at Penhallow you went out with your bucket and stool and milked them where you found them, we set off now in search. At the other end of the paddock from Rupert's house, a sandy track wound out onto the burrows, and as the gate was never shut, the cows quite frequently went out there to graze. We soon found them, cudding quietly beside one of the unexpected pools of clear water that lie in the sandy hallows, and, being used to the system, they made no attempt to move away as we came up to them.

They were Herefords, the Penhallow cows, and there were three of them. Big, red animals, with mild white faces, and spectacle marks round their eyes, they may not have given a tremendous amount of milk—but it was enough, and the quality was excellent.

I milked Priscilla, the doyenne of the herd—the others were Dawn, her daughter, like her but smaller, and Hawthorn, who was darker red, and had a rather blotchy face. Mrs. Evans wiped their hairy udders with a cloth, and a drop of water that she had brought in one of the buckets. Then she settled me down on my stool, in the approved position, at Priscilla's flank, and herself milked Dawn and Hawthorn.

Pressing my brow into the cow's springy, sweet-smelling side, I squinted down at my hands. Priscilla had big, easy teats, and, squeezing as I had been shown, I managed to get quite a good series of squirts of milk into my bucket. Mrs. Evans's hands went like clockwork, and the sharp zing! zing! of the first jets into the bucket was soon muffled by the fine head of creamy foam that a good milker whips up. I laboured on, every inch of milk a triumph. How my forearms ached, after a few minutes. I felt the strength go out of my grip, and changed to the other two teats in the hope that the slight shift of position would ease the strain. Mrs. Evans had finished both of her cows before I had wrested Priscilla's half-gallon or so from her, and she tactfully suggested that she might as well take over for the last bit. 'Most of the cream is in the strippings, Libby—and we don't want to leave that behind, indeed!'

When all was done, Mrs. Evans poured all the milk into one bucket, and we set off to walk back to the farm. The sun was in

12

our faces now, and our long shadows streamed out behind us as we walked, breathing in the sweet steam that rose from the warm new milk. Larks sprang, singing, into the dazzling light; gulls hung, mewing, over the edge of the sea and here and there at our feet were clusters of mushrooms. We picked them as we walked, zigzagging from one good clump to another, and carried them home in the empty bucket. Saturday's to Wednesday's mushrooms might appear on the breakfast table, but Thursday's and Friday's went with Mrs. Evans to the market, where she had a stall.

Trotting along with my eyes on the ground, looking for mushrooms, I was constantly discovering the most beautiful wild flowers. Some of them I knew, but even they looked somehow different here. Harebells, for instance. We had harebells at home—we saw them when we went for picnics in the Yorkshire dales. But there they grew singly—individual flags of blue, nodding here and there on the sheep-nibbled limestone. Here they grew in swathes—pools, sheets, breadths of blue, that you came upon, all unexpectedly, as you topped the crest of one of the little rolling hills of the burrows.

The arable fields too had their own flowers, some of which seemed wonderfully exotic. The pimpernel was a favourite, both for its curious faded red petals and for its magical ability to foretell the weather—but the little darling of all was the heartsease or wild pansy. Perhaps I am wrong in calling it the heartsease, for it was certainly not the gawky, straggly, microcephalic offering that goes by that name in this locality, all stem and no flower. The Penhallow wild pansies were like perfect miniatures of garden pansies, yellow, and with neat black cats'-whisker markings all round their faces. We found them growing both in stubbles and in old pastures, and we loved them exceedingly. They could have been Mountain pansies, perhaps.

Chicory was an astonishment to town-reared children. With its round daisy face and innocent purity of colour it still seems to me a very desirable plant. The wonder is that no plant breeder has ever taken it up and developed it into a first-class border plant. Not that it needs much alteration. It only needs to be made a little bigger and less straggly to be worth a bit of

13

anybody's border room. The colour is heavenly (literally) already; nobody could improve that.

But it was not the chicory that was the most magic flower of Penhallow. This was a small plant, with relatively large trumpet-shaped flowers, delicately scented. Its pale yellow petals looked more fragile than silk, as if the merest puff of wind would blow them away, and it grew in a field beside a cart-track, under the lee of a wind-carved blackthorn hedge which curved over it like a breaking wave arrested in mid-fall. It was not like any other wild-flower I had ever seen before. Could it be the Lily of the Field? I asked. Mrs. Evans did not think so. What it was, of course, was the Evening Primrose, and I now have the pleasure of growing it here and there all over the place, for it is a most generous self-seeder.

There were nasty plants at Penhallow as well as the ones we liked—plants that stung, or tore you, or stuck you up with their seeds, or stank if they were bruised. Ragwort was one of these. Head-high, rank and poisonous, it grew in drifts on the burrows, and anywhere else where it could find a foothold. The air in August was full of its floating seeds. We children had a name for anything floating in the air—we called them Eureth Beasties —and a high proportion of the Beastie count was provided by the ragwort.

But if you wanted to find a ragwort plant on Penhallow today, you would have to search for a long time. The sheep have eaten them all out. It is a curious fact that ragwort, so poisonous to cattle and horses, does not affect sheep at all, and, during the winter, when they are scavenging around for food, they love to make a succulent mouthful of the hearts of the plants. Being bitten to the ground every time it rears its head does not suit the ragwort's life-style, and it soon fades away.

Back in the 1930s there were no sheep on Penhallow. Mr. Evans told us that he had brought several lots of ewes, but that on each occasion they had been killed by becoming infected with liver-fluke. The factor that tipped the balance was the discovery of the medicinal properties of carbon tetrachloride. When this became commercially available, farmers, by regular dosing, were able to control liver fluke, and sheep now thrive on Penhallow as well as on any other farm. 'And thus do we

14

see,' as Feste remarked, 'how the whirligig of Time brings in his revenges.'

When we got back to the farmhouse we carried our pails of milk and mushrooms into the dairy. How well I remember that room! Dim, square, stone-floored, its window was made of fly-proof metal gauze instead of glass, and the rain that came in was enough to keep the place as damp and cool as a cellar. And what richness was there! What a wealth of provision! Rabbits, with glazed eyes, hung by their hindlegs, from pegs in the walls. A big churn stood in one corner, and the wire meatsafe in another, with the remains of yesterday's massive leg of lamb in it. The big stone table in the middle of the room was laden with food. Two cakes, freshly baked by Gladys, were cooling on a wire tray; a basket brimmed with eggs, brown, white and speckled, adorned with a feather or two. Two or three pounds of waxy yellow butter, fresh from the churn and beaded with water, reposed on a plate—and jugs of cream, crocks of mush-rooms, a brace of neatly-trussed chickens and a big damson pie jostled for the rest of the space. A large punnet of potatoes, freshly dug, and still damp with sandy earth, gleamed like golden nuggets in the shadows, and the subdued purple of young swedes added its note of colour to the picture. Hams and sides of bacon, glittering with salt, hung from hooks in the ceiling.

The scent of the dairy formed its own complex bouquet too, the low, earthy smells of the vegetables and the rabbits rising through the cakes and butter to the top note of the new-milk smell that we had just brought in. Mrs. Evans poured the milk through a strainer, and then set it to cool in a broad earthen-ware pan which she put on the shelf.

The milk 'set', as Mrs. Evans called it, the next thing was to feed the animals. Dawn and Hawthorn both had calves, which were kept in the buildings, and which were still being fed on the bucket. They got some of the milk left over from yesterday, from which the cream had been skimmed for butter making. It was warmed up with a drop of boiling water from the big black kettle, always simmering on the hob, and mixed to a fine gruel with a couple of handfuls of barley meal, stirred in with a stick. We took the buckets in to them in their dim, hay-scented

15

cot, and they thrust their faces in and slurped it back with a right good will. They were not new calves by now, but a month or two old, and you could feel the horn buds growing under the skin above their ears. They liked to be scratched round there, and would push their little hard heads at you for more, while their long, sticky tongues looped out and tried to gather up some part of your clothing to suck. But we could not linger over the calves, for the other animals were waiting.

The pigs were next. Outside the back door, Gladys had put a white enamel pail that held the day's scraps. Bread, custard, potato peelings, tea-leaves—even—a little brutally—bacon-rinds, all went in, with a good soak of boiling water on top of them. Mrs. Evans added a nicely-judged slop of milk and some more water, and then scooped in barley meal until the pail was full. Then she stirred it up with a stick. It smelled quite savoury.

The pig-cote, where the sow lived with her litter, was at one end of the little stone-built barn, and I took good care to get well behind Mrs. Evans as we approached the door. Even she had provided herself with a stout stick, and as we paused by the door before lifting the latch, you could easily tell why. The pigs had heard us coming, and were now in full cry, bumping against the door shrieking and clamouring for their breakfast like a hell full of tormented demons.

Mrs. Evans grasped her stick, and raised the bucket of swill high. Then, slipping up the latch, she strode in. Shouting for order, and laying about her with her stick, she charged down the seething mob, and hastily slopped a good helping of the steaming brew into the trough. Instantly there was silence—or as near as you can get to silence when eleven pigs are competitively slurping and golloping. She regarded them for a moment or two, with pride, and then withdrew. The pigs made no effort to follow, and she was able to shut the door again with no difficulty. For the time being they were totally pre-occupied.

Rupert's helping was still in the bucket, but as you could pour the swill into his trough over the wall, feeding him was not half so hair-raising. Sometimes he would get his front feet up on the wall, and his yellow tusks and savage little eyes looked dangerous, but a tap on the snout with the stick soon

16

sent him squealing and scuttling away and once he got his trotters in the trough, he was as greedy as any piglet.

With the pigs behind us, we turned to the poultry. They were still in their houses, and before we let them out, we went into the barn to get them a bucketful of grain. It was lovely in the barn. The mill which crushed or ground the grain, according to the setting, was against the back wall, and the cool sweet smell of the T.V.O. (tractor vaporising oil) that drove its motor mingled with the slightly astringent flouriness of the grain smell in a perfect blend that seemed the exact olfactory counterpart of the barn's cobwebs and mysterious shadows. The mysterious atmosphere of the barn was augmented by the fact that we were not allowed to go up the ladder into the loft. Not that we particularly yearned to; what was downstairs was good enough to be going on with. For as well as the mill and the oil-drum, there were various corn-bins standing round the walls, and the contents of each were delightful. There was a bin of oats for the horses—long, slim grains with pale shiny coats hiding a hard, silky-haired grain. Then there was a barrel of barley meal, with a round metal scoop in it, from which Mrs. Evans made the pig-food. And finally there was the unmilled barley, hard and bright, with its little plump grains— and having filled a certain battered bucket to the brim with it, we went off to bring the morning into the poultry houses.

The hens and turkeys were in one big house; the geese and ducks in another smaller one. Alone, I was rather afraid of the geese and turkeys, who stretched out their long necks and hissed or gobbled at you in a way which was very daunting when you were only three feet six tall. But, with Mrs. Evans, there was no need to be afraid. Nothing could hurt you.

Out rushed the poultry at the opening of their houses, and fell upon the grain which we flung in wide rainbow arcs over the dewy grass of the paddock. It was fun to watch them scrambling for it, the young flibbertigibbet cockerels always sure that the latest handful must be the best, while the more sedate and experienced hens stayed on the patch they'd started on, and carefully scratched and picked it over.

With all the poultry out and foraging, it was a good time to go in and collect the eggs. The hen-house was a low building, spanned in several directions by sagging perches, and you crawled beneath them to get at the nests. Feathers and hen-smelling dust got up your nose and made you sneeze as you groped for the eggs, lying, warm and smooth, in the strawy nests. The hens were a motley crowd, and the eggs too varied greatly in size and colour. There were brown ones, speckled ones, and a few large ones of brilliant chalk white. There were enough almost to fill the grain bucket most mornings—I handed them back to Mrs. Evans, then crawled out backwards under-neath the perches, and we took them back to the dairy. Occa-sionally there would be a hen on a nest who would fluff out her feathers, scold and peck at your hand if you offered to slip it beneath her. But Mrs. Evans would never let me feel for eggs under any sitting hens. 'Don't disturb her, Libby; or per-haps tomorrow she'll go away and make a nest somewhere else,' she would say.

For in spite of the nest boxes, some of the hens did 'lay away'. We had a regular round of known places to look—in the hay-passage by the calves' pen, in a hollowed-out nest at the foot of the haystack in the rickyard; behind an old sack that hung from the workbench in the cart-shed, and so on. In addition to these there was always the chance of a bonanza. Coming back from milking, perhaps, your eye might be caught by a gleam in the hedgerow, and there, concealed by a tuft of bracken or the leaves of a giant burdock, would be anything from ten to twenty-four eggs—a clutch that a hen was hoping to incu-bate privily. But Mrs. Evans didn't believe in the dangers of hedgerow sitting and we would take up the clutch, giving each egg a good shake first to see if it was addled. If you felt the inside of the egg slopping to and fro as you shook, you knew it was no good, and threw it into the further field. If the hen was actually discovered sitting on the eggs, she was transferred to a safe coop near the house; but the fact that many of these stolen clutches *were* addled seems to indicate that most of the hens had failed to sit properly. Occasionally some exceptionally cunning mother would outwit us, and would arrive back one day proudly conducting four or five tiny cheeping morsels of black or yellow fluff. But no hedge sitter ever brought off a brood really worth having.

18

The real clutches, the on-purpose ones, were in coops with little runs attached in the little gone-by orchard at the back of the farm. By August all the eggs would be hatched, so we never had the pleasure of witnessing the hatching. But some of the broods were still quite young, and we could help to give them their feed soaked in milk, and see that the mothers clucking in their coops had their scatter of grain and their pot of fresh water twice a day. Young chickens develop at a tremendous pace, and before the end of a month the tiny downy babies, so innocent and sweet-looking, had become scrawny half-fledged adolescents, almost ready to join their older brothers and sisters in the pleasures of the dung-heap and the dust-bath around the yard.

Our feelings towards the hens were ambivalent. Each of us had adopted one which we called our own. Gillian's was a large light reddish-brown hen and mine a smaller black one, slightly lame. Richard had chosen one of the young cockerels that were being reared for the table—a splendid creature, with warm buff feathers, and a dazzling beetle-green tail. Yet though we liked the hens, we had no objection to meeting them, beautifully browned, on the serving-dish at lunch-time, and we liked it when Gladys let us help her pluck the victims—giving us the easy bits, like the breasts and the backs to do. The feathers pulled out so extraordinarily sweetly, and the body underneath it felt damp, warm and doughy, like new bread. Actually, being hens, Gillian's and mine were never sacrificed, but Richard's was. 'What are we having for dinner today?' we asked Mrs. Evans nearly every day—and then one day she said it. 'We're having Richard's cock today!' Poor Mrs. Evans! How she blushed! So did Richard. There must have been something about Richard that made him subject to this sort of thing, for years later a new French au pair girl earned herself a place in our family dictionary of quotations when she said to him at dinner, 'Richard, will you please pass water?'

As well as eating Richard's cock, we would usually be regaled during our month at Penhallow with at least one duck dinner, and one goose one. Most of the geese, like the turkeys, were intended for the Christmas trade on Mrs. Evans's market stall, but there always seemed to be one big enough to provide us with our treat, and as the geese were invariably hostile to us

19

children, waddling along in pursuit of us, with their deep bellies trailing on the grass and their cold, pale eyes fixed in an inimical stare, we didn't mind one of them being killed.

The ducks, a mixture of white Aylesburys and brown Khaki Campbells, spent most of their time on a large pond that lay between the main range of farm buildings and the barn. One side of the pond shelved up to the green grass of the paddock; the other was bounded by the wall of the rickyard. Pink persicaria grew lavishly in the rickyard and out of the wall; trodden on, it had a very characteristic smell, and you could easily have told, with your eyes shut, that you were near the duckpond.

The odd man out among the ducks was Pongo, the Muscovy drake. Instead of consorting with the others as they dabbled and upended themselves on the pond's green water, he preferred to keep himself to himself. His chosen territory was the broad cobbled path that separated the cowshed and stable range from the long, narrow muck-heap. Fairly far apart along the building wall were two taps, one for drinking water, one not. Big tubs stood beneath these to catch any drips, and here Pongo was usually to be found. He rarely got into the tubs and swam; he preferred to sit on the edge, ducking his head constantly into the water and directing lucent trickles of it back over his piebald shoulders. Then he would preen himself, and turning round to face the other way, would defecate squirtily into the tub. And then he would wag his tail and look back over his shoulder with the utmost self-satisfaction. We children thought he was wonderful.

By the time we had been round all these animals, it would be breakfast time. After two hours or more of activity in the open air, I would be good and ready for it and it was worth being ready for, for breakfast at Penhallow was in the nature of a feast.

We didn't have porridge, for one thing. Not that I had anything against porridge; on the contrary, I liked it and still do. But at home, the porridge would only be followed by an egg in some guise—boiled, poached or scrambled. Bacon, for some reason, was considered to be unsuitable for small children in those days, so the presence of porridge automatically meant the absence of bacon in my simple mind.

But at Penhallow, where there was no porridge, we had bacon. We ate together, children and grown-ups, and so of course we ate the same food. And the festive atmosphere that this induced was augmented by the presence of one of our favourite pairs of aunt and uncle. Every year my father's sister, Phyllis, and her husband, George, spent a good part of the month with us, and so the eight of us would all sit down round the big table and eat bacon together.

And not just little squinny bits of bacon such as we see nowadays. No, indeed! The lavishness of the Penhallow bacon recalled the old Somerset wassailing song—'Hats full, caps full, three bushel bags full'. Two big meat dishes were borne in every morning, one covered with bacon, and the other one plated with fried eggs, overlapping like tiles on a roof, and all speckly brown from basting with the salty fat that had run from the home-cured bacon. And there was never any question of sending in 'enough'. Gladys always made sure that she sent in too much, so that at the end when everybody had eaten as much as they could hold—the children one egg each, the women two, and the men three or even four—there would still be two or three eggs on the dish looking for a home.

A pause for a smoke, for digestion, and indeed elimination was necessary after this gargantuan meal, and one after another the grown-ups could be observed slipping away to the two lava-tories that stood upright and dignified beneath the gnarled damson trees in the orchard.

To some extent these lavatories resembled the ones immortal-ised by Charles Sale in *The Specialist*, and at first I thought the grown-ups were talking quite seriously when I heard them comparing the relative merits of spool or bobbin door-fastenings, or discussing the disconcertingness of apples (or damsons) dropping on the roof. It was years later that I recognised their remarks, retrospectively, as quotations. But in point of fact the Penhallow lavatories differed from *The Specialist*'s in several important details.

They were not unisex, for one thing. Women used the older one, nearer the house, whose crimson paint had weathered to a soft, glowing pink. Men went to the shiny new aluminium one down at the bottom of the orchard, where the bracken nodded

21

over the old stone dyke. Another difference from the American models was that these were not just holes in the ground, but emptiable drums with wooden seats over them. You had a carton of nice pink carbolic powder to sprinkle into the drum, and instead of a mail-order catalogue, torn up squares of newspaper hung, conveniently available, on a nail. The nicest touch of all was a goose-wing—not put there to out-Rabelais Rabelais, but to flick the dust and cobwebs off the ledges and corners that the exigencies of the construction had left on the inside.

While the grown-ups passed before us in stately procession, we children played around and waited for the second half of the day to get under way. There was always something to do. Big planks of wood, the cut ends soaked all soft and furry from the sea, were often washed up on the beach, and the Evans family would fetch them up and stack them handy by the house until they came in useful for something. We were inclined at first to regard every plank as evidence of a tragic shipwreck, but Mr. Evans soon scotched that idea. Deck cargo, he said— badly stacked on some little tramp steamer, washing overboard as she wallowed along in rough seas somewhere up the Irish Channel. Our father arranged some of the deck cargo planks to make us an aeroplane, and we often got into it for a quick flight after breakfast.

Then I had my other bit of milking to attend to. Little plants of sunspurge grew thickly along the bottom of the wall between the garden and the paddock, and I spent many happy minutes breaking off their tips and collecting the thick milky sap in a cockleshell. It wasn't exactly *for* anything, it was just nice in itself, and when it all turned brown and congealed you just dropped the shell and forgot all about it. There was never any shortage of 'cows', however many I picked and despoiled.

The other little job that fitted in very well after breakfast was to get out my stable full of horses, and air and admire them. The stable was a shoe box, with carefully cut windows and half-doors, and the horses were feathers. I knew very well that to other people they were only feathers, but to me they were something more. They were symbols of horses—outward and visible signs of inward and spiritual horses, as you might say— and in my imagination I gave each horse the attributes of colour

22

and personality that his representative feather seemed to suggest. My big grey was a seagull's pinion, and I endowed him with a satin skin, and a fine, noble personality. Next to him in the stable stood a thin-legged, well-bred chestnut, who must, I think, in retrospect, have come from a kestrel. Two or three hearty bays owed an obvious allegiance to the farmyard Rhode Island Reds; and pride of all was a delicate cream, only a pony, preened from the underneath of a passing swallow.

But when Geoff, the farmhand, came by with a couple of halters over his arm, I hastily shoved my beauties in their stable and ran after him.

Geoff was a sandy-haired man with light blue eyes, who worked at Penhallow for many years. He lived in a bungalow up the field—only he always pronounced it as if it was the other kind of bung, the beer-barrel kind, withholding the hard 'g'. He had two children of his own, younger than us, so I suppose he was used to prattle. At any rate, he never seemed to mind if all three of us came with him when he went to catch up the horses.

There were three horses, Prince, Duchess and Darling. They were typical Welsh cart horses, dark bay-brown in colour, and rather less than sixteen hands in height. They may not have had the majestic presence of the big shires and clydesdales we saw working about the streets at home, but they were strong and active, and (like nearly everything else at Penhallow) kind to children.

Prince was everybody's favourite, and quite often, if he was the only one being caught up, we would all three ride home on his back together. Duchess and Darling sometimes had foals at foot, so they only had to work on big occasions like reaping, or carting corn. Single horse jobs were done by Prince. Mr. Evans was very fond of him too, and told us a story about him. 'We were earthing up some potatoes, just Prince and me, one morning in the spring. And when I came to the end of the row, I thought I'd stop for a cigarette. So I turned Prince round, ready for the next row, got my packet out, and lit up. And the way the wind was blowing, I had to turn my back to him to get it alight. And when I looked round again—there he was, lying down between the rows, with his harness on and everything! So

I said to him, "Oh, Prince! Are you really as tired as that? Well, so am I then! We'll go home!" and we did!'

One year after a grey stallion had travelled the district Duchess and Darling both had grey foals. One was light grey and one was dark; their names were Wallace and Windsor. Everybody petted them, and they were perfectly tame and friendly, but Mr. Evans never found time to halter-break them before they were sold—and there is a world of difference, for a young horse, between being stroked and petted in a field, and having a halter put on your head and being tied up. 'Pulling' is the word they use in Wales to describe the lesson a young horse is taught the first time he is tied up, and many young horses make a good deal of fuss about it.

Wallace was sold off the farm, and taken away in a cattle-lorry, so his ignorance of the halter didn't matter; but, having had no offers for Windsor, Mr. Evans decided to take him to a horse fair. They loaded him into the horse-box by joining hands under his rump and hustling him up the ramp, and when he arrived at the fair, he made no difficulty about clattering down again. Mr. Evans tied him up, and there he stood, a fine picture of an iron-grey colt, with large, intelligent eyes, and ears pricked sharply at the new strange noises about him. Luckily, he was so absorbed that he clearly never realised that he was tied. So handsome did he look that before long a buyer came up, and after looking in his mouth and feeling his legs, offered Mr. Evans a better price than he had ever hoped to get. They struck hands on the bargain in the time-honoured way, and the buyer turned away to fetch his pony and trap for the homeward journey. Then he turned back. 'By the way—I hope he's been pulled?' he said. Mr. Evans's heart gave a guilty jump. But the price was good, and he didn't want to lose the sale on a techni-cality, so to speak. So he put on a bold front and took a chance. 'Pulled? I should say so!' he answered airily. 'Nearly pulled his blinking head off!'

'So then he tied him to the back of the trap,' he told us afterwards, 'and put the pony into a trot. And when Windsor felt the halter pull on his head, I thought to myself—now, look out for fireworks! But he was as good as gold. Off he went behind that trap, throwing out his feet—one-two, one-two—like one of those trotters—for all the world as if he'd had a halter on his head every day of his life! But I was glad to see them get out of sight!'

We did not mourn the passing of Wallace and Windsor. Prince was still there, and that was what mattered. How I loved to be hoisted up onto his back, warm and silky—to tangle my fingers in the coarse, greasy hairs of his mane, to smell his horse smell, sweeter than any other, and to swing to his rolling gait as he plodded obediently along behind Geoff or Mr. Evans. Sometimes I was allowed to ride him when he was wearing his harness. Then I would fit myself in between the collar and the big heavy cart saddle, and grasp the hames to steady myself. If he was to work in chains rather than between shafts, he would not be wearing the saddle, but only a flat strap of leather across his back, and then there was room for all of us. Of course we were not on his back while he was actually working, but only on the way to or from the field where the work was.

Another pleasure was to go in the flat cart which was used for little jobs about the place. Driftwood might need fetching up from the beach, or a load of cut marram-grass for rick-thatching. Or there might be a load of coal, or a sack or two of flour to get from the village. It was on an errand to the village with Prince and Geoff that I suffered one of the sharpest humiliations of my life. I was on my way to the pink lavatory when I saw Geoff come out of the house, jump onto the cart to which Prince was harnessed and set off over the burrows, towards the lane that led to the village. My errand forgotten, I flew after him. 'Can I come? Can I come?' 'Yes, of course!' and in a minute I was up beside him on the front of the cart, as happy as a king. I was oblivious of my needs on the way to the village too, distracting myself with my own chatter, getting Geoff to show me how to hold the reins, and asking about Prince's shoes—why was one shinier than the other? Where did he go to have new shoes put on? How often? and so on. But when we had gone into Mrs. George's shop, the pangs returned with an urgency that almost amounted to crisis. Geoff had bought whatever he had come for, but he and Mrs. George were talking. How they talked! Minute after interminable minute dragged by, and still they went on, while I, too shy to utter, knotted my knees in agony in the background. And then—oh shame! I reached and passed my holding-point. I felt a disgraceful hot trickle down my leg—but nobody noticed it! So I had to plumb the depths of chagrin by inter-rupting the grown-up conversation and announcing in a small voice, 'I'm going to the lavatory!' That set the cat among the pigeons all right. Mrs. George, with a very black look for which I can hardly blame her, went for a cloth—and Geoff said, quite crossly for him, 'Why didn't you say you wanted to go, and Mrs. George would've took you to the lavatory?' I hung my head and couldn't reply—and to this day I still don't really know why I couldn't bring myself to ask.

I felt very subdued on the way home, and very self-conscious about my wet shorts. But luckily nobody was about, and I was able to creep upstairs and extract a clean pair from the suitcase. Not knowing what to do with the wet ones I folded them up small, and put them in a corner of the bedroom near the com-mode. I suppose Nurse must have found them and guessed my guilty secret, but she never said anything to me about it. Nurse was nice like that—you could rely on her. Geoff, too, seemed to regard the incident as closed, and after a while I recovered most of my self-esteem.

When I wasn't tagging round after Geoff or Mrs. Evans I could sometimes go with Mr. Evans on his rounds. When the tide was right, he would set a net overnight for fish. We would walk down when the tide was out in the evening, and fasten a long net to a row of green, crooked, barnacled posts striding out to sea. In my mind's eye, I see the posts as tall as trees, and the net as long as a tennis net, but I dare say that was the effect of my diminutive stature. Then, in the morning early, we would go down again. The tide had been in and gone out again by then, and a number of fish would have been left stranded in the net. They were small plaice, about eight inches long, with strange ugly half-sideways heads and pretty red spots on their backs. They would have one mesh of the net caught in one gill, and I used to wonder why they were so stupid about getting away when it appeared that a most trifling bit of back-and-forward wriggling would have set them free. We never found them difficult to detach, anyway; there they hung, like fruit on a tree just waiting to be gathered. We would collect them up, cool, firm and smelling of the sea, and rush back to the farm with them, and Gladys, who was Mrs. Evans' sister, would fry them for our breakfast. I have never eaten fish as delicious as those little Penhallow plaice. Crispy brown, piled on the great meat-dish, they would come to the table with plate after plate of delicious thin bread and butter, and the tender white flesh crumbled off the bones in a miracle of delectable freshness. Gladys was a beautiful cook.

She was a good bread-and-butter cutter, too. Like all Welsh women she held the loaf against her bosom, and cut towards herself. I have never liked to try this method myself; the consequences of a slip seem too awful to risk. But Gladys never cut herself—and, furthermore, she kept the edge of the loaf straight too.

One day at tea-time, the sight of two plates of her beautiful thin bread inspired my father and my uncle to have a bread-and-butter eating race. Slices were counted—the champions squared up into position, standing up, one each side of the big table— then, at the drop of a handkerchief—they were off! Speechless with excitement, hands clasped in ecstasy, we three children stood at the end of the table and watched them. How red they were! How the veins on their temples swelled as they crammed their cheeks even to bursting point! How their Adam's apples bobbed up and down as they gulped and masticated! In truth, they gained, not lost, in majesty in such moments of frivolity. Even so did the Greek Gods descend, sportively, to the plains where ordinary mortals pursued their humdrum avocations. I do not remember who won the great bread-and-butter race, but I remember as if it was yesterday the dazzling, the awe-inspiring sense of *permitted* lèse majesté, and the retrospective glow, as if great beings had for once descended to our level, and sanctified it.

Mrs. Evans was almost exactly the same age as my mother, Gladys a few years younger. Both had black hair, but whereas Mrs. Evans was little, with a sweet smile, a gentle manner and hazel eyes, Gladys was tall and dark-eyed. She had an extremely upright bearing, and rather a noble look. I always imagined that Boadicea or Hippolyta might have looked rather like her; I could easily imagine her driving a chariot, or sitting, like

Britannia, in a crested helm, with spear and shield at the ready. She had a clear, incisive tone, and a slight stutter, a combination which made everything she said very individual. There was a certain dryness in her comments, and as I got to know her better, after I was grown up, I always felt that she saw further into things than most people do. When we were little, Gladys did virtually all the cooking for the family and the visitors, turning out a succession of delicious meals on nothing more sophisticated than a kitchen fire and a twin-burner oil stove. Mrs. Evans did the outside jobs, feeding the animals and running the market stall every Friday. But in later years, after the war, the roles seemed to be reversed, and Gladys had a large part in the care of the Penhallow sheep. I can see her now, leaning on her tall stick, the wind flapping her macintosh round her legs, sending Queen, the smooth black-and-tan sheep dog, after a puckle of ewes that had strayed too far towards the cliff-edge; there was an elemental quality about her, a kind of native grandeur; she seemed in scale with the big forces of out-of-doors, the gale-force winds, and the seas smashing in white foam high on the rocks.

In her later years she successfully became both a gardener and a beekeeper, which all adds to the evidence for her special quality of insight, these both being hobbies which produce much more than just honey and flowers.

Mr. Evans (I was supposed to call him Jack after I was grown up, but it always felt slightly cheeky and I continued to think of him as Mr. Evans) was an eminently sociable man—Dr. Johnson would have called him a 'clubbable' man. He was an excellent raconteur; he held himself very upright, with his head back rather stiffly, and his chin tucked in; his cap was always well down over his nose, and he would shoot you such a glance from under the brim, with twinkling, light-blue eyes in a long, brown face—that you were ready to laugh before the story even started. 'Droll' is the word that sums up his conversational style for me.

He had been a farrier in the army in the Great War, and had suffered many hardships in the desert campaigns. We loved to hear about this—how they had had to go without water for so long that everybody's tongue had become blackened, and swollen to twice its normal size. And then, when they finally succeeded in making their way back to their own lines, how they were only allowed half a cup of water each at first, lest it should make them vomit, and dehydrate them even further.

He liked to tease us too sometimes; and sometimes we fell for it, and sometimes we didn't. One evening he was taking Prince out to pasture, the three of us perched, as usual, on his back. Coming to a closed gate, Mr. Evans climbed over it without a word, then, holding the halter over the gate, said encouragingly to Prince, 'Come on, boy! Jump!' Richard and I, to our shame, began to wail to get down, but Gillian was made of sterner stuff. 'Go on—make him jump!' she cried. 'I'll sit him!'

Another part of Mr. Evans's round had to do with those pathetic bundles of glazed-eyed rabbits that hung in the dairy. We who live in the post-myxomatosis era have to a large extent forgotten the frightful havoc wrought by rabbits in the old days. Breeding madly—a doe is physiologically capable of conceiving again within one day of having a litter—eating voraciously and fouling with their droppings even more than they eat, rabbits swarming unchecked could make many light land farms virtually unworkable. It was war to the knife between the farmer and the rabbit, although the value of the trapped rabbits in the market did make it into something of a love-hate relationship.

Some farmers in South Wales called upon the services of professional trappers, but Mr. Evans went after the rabbits himself. He had various methods of catching them. A double-barrelled shotgun hung on the wall over the kitchen fireplace, and lovely red spent cartridge cases with brass ends could be picked up in the fields and on the burrows. We didn't exactly pick them up for anything; they were just nice in themselves, like acorns or conkers. When they had lost their crispness through being carried around in a shorts pocket for a week or two, they were discarded.

Then there were the ferrets. These lived in a cage near the house, and I was afraid of them because I had been warned that if I poked my fingers in through the wire they would bite them *right off!* They were white and slinky, with fierce pink eyes. When Mr. Evans put their dish of bread and milk in the cage,

29

they coiled about with an air of deadly self-sufficiency that did nothing to endear them to me. Occasionally they were put in a sack, which heaved in a sinister way, and taken out to do their work, but we children never went on one of these expeditions.

The other members of the team were three greyhounds, Tim, a rangy brindle, Sam, who was fawn, and Nip, white, with grey patches. I think the greyhounds must have been fastened up for part of the time; they did not seem to be always around, like pretty, gentle Fan, the sheepdog, and Puppy, the trembling, senile, half-blind terrier, who was sixteen years old.

The most fruitful method of catching rabbits, however was not by net or gun, but by snaring, and nearly every evening Mr. Evans would set off with a bundle of the wicked-looking dark gold wires hanging out of his pocket. In the morning he would go round again to pick up the catch. Sometimes we would go with him. We were aware of a certain ambivalence in our attitude to the whole business. Rabbits had to be killed if the farm was to go on. That was self-evident. And it was 'soppy' to be afraid of death as such. We knew instinctively that too much display of emotion on the subject would be bad form, and would lower us in the eyes of Mr. Evans, whom we so much looked up to. But still an uneasy inner voice would revolt against some of the things we saw. A rabbit that pulls the wire tight around its neck strangles itself to death in a minute or two, but some of the smaller ones had slipped half way through, and were caught round the waist. These had either died slowly, struggling frantically, as evidenced by the awful circle of flattened bare earth around them, or were still alive when morning came. I know what I think about snares now, but then I took the easy way out. Mr. Evans said it was all right, and Mr. Evans was my hero, who could do no wrong. Ergo, it must be all right. I must say that everybody did set snares in those days, and indeed I think it is still legal now. I personally think it is a nasty business, and would never set one or allow one to be set on my land. But, of course, we don't have to contend with the same problems that faced Mr. Evans, farming as we do in totally different circumstances.

Our parents were great walkers, in the tradition of those days, and on the days when they were setting off on their twenty-odd miles, we stayed behind with Nurse and played around the farm for most of the day. When the tide was right, we would go down for a swim, but the lovely, lonely beaches were so close to the farm that it didn't need to assume the proportions of an expedition. Those beaches had absolutely everything. There was a cave, gloomy, cold, and damp which the sea filled right up at high tide; there were rock pools, with shrimps and crabs, and red or green sea anemones, like half-sucked wine-gums glued to the rocks, there were big lumps of rock sticking up out of the sand, with curved moats excavated around them by the swing and suck of the retreating tide; and there was the sand itself— miles of it. Here and there were long tidal pools, shelving depressions about eighteen inches deep and a hundred yards long, where the water was always warm, and where we could end- lessly dabble and sail our boats. Richard's was *Prince Edward,* and mine was *Sea-Lion,* and we had saved up our pocket money and bought them in the village at Mrs. George's shop—pre- sumably when I had become persona grata once more! They were ordinary enough when we got them, Bermuda-rigged, with sails fixed rigidly fore and aft, but our uncle kindly modified them for us and made them capable of sailing much more like real boats. Of course, even then, there was no way of making them tack, except when a chance squall of wind caused them to gybe. *Prince Edward* did not last long. Put down casually on the seat in the porch one day, she fell to the floor, and was acciden- tally trodden on and dismasted. But *Sea-Lion* survived many a trip across the pools, and even a few hair-raising voyages into the choppy reaches of the open sea.

We did not often make big sand-castles in the bucket-and- spade tradition. Instead, we developed a technique of our own, which made smaller, but much more fantastic erections. You chose a place about half-way down the beach, and scooped a little hole in the sand, until you reached water level, and the bottom of the hole was all sloppy and swimmy. This was your quarry, and by picking up handfuls of this wet sand and letting it dribble out of the back of your hand, you could shape real arabian-nights-type bowers. Crockets, pinnacles, flying buttresses piled up in a sort of Gothic extravaganza, and if you were careful, you could end up with something rather like the

Martyrs' Memorial in Oxford. Then you beautified it with shells, feathers, dried foam, dead sand-shrimps, coloured sea-weed, or whatever else took your fancy from the endless variety of jetsam in the broad, humming, hopping band of the high-tide mark, further up the beach.

Thus the morning passed pleasantly, and at one o'clock we would gather our gear and trudge through the soft dune sand back to the farm, where Gladys would be setting our dinner at one end of the big table in our sitting-room. Sniffing the air as we cast our bathing costumes to dry on the big stones of the garden wall, we would try to guess what was in store for us today. Veal and forcemeat? Chicken? And then to follow, perhaps a creamy macaroni pudding and sliced peaches! They were happy days.

Sometimes my father would spend a few hours sketching, which he did with great skill, and then the rest of us might all go down to the beach together. Our grown-ups did not go in much for sun-bathing; between swims, they would entertain themselves by improvising a putting-course, taking it in turns with an old club and a gone-by golf-ball; or if the wind was cold, they might warm up after a bathe with a vigorous game of leapfrog. This had its own dangers. Once, when they were staying at Rhossili, before we knew about Penhallow, Uncle George got his ankle broken at this wild sport. My mother was the 'back' on that occasion, and he was the 'frog', but through some error of timing she stood up just as he was in mid-leap, causing him to o'erleap himself and fall on the other with shattering effect. With two doctors present, it didn't take long to realise that the ankle was probably broken, and it was soon bound up and splinted into a rigid position. The only remaining problem was how to get him up the cliff? At that end of the beach the only way up was by a narrow, deeply sunken sandy path that wound and zig-zagged up so steeply that you often had to use hands as well as feet. Any kind of stretcher or piggy-back was out of the question. At last he decided there was only one way for him to get up—on his bottom, backwards. 'I don't want to spoil your day,' he said, considerately. 'You go off and have your bathe and your picnic, and I'll spend the day getting up here at my own pace. I'll see you at the top, at about five

32

o'clock!' And he did. Those cliffs are used for hang gliding now. It seems they must be fated to be associated with these dangerous forms of sport.

George was a splendid uncle, although you had to be careful he didn't catch you early in the morning and give you a dose of 'chin pie'. You don't hear about chin pie these days—that classic torture inflicted by uncles who, laughing terrifyingly, seized their young nephews and nieces, and rubbed cheeks with them—always first thing in the morning, when twenty-four hours' worth of beard rasped against the victim's tender cheeks. One always laughed, shriekingly, fearing to be considered wet; but actually it hurt quite a lot. Perhaps it went out with the advent of the electric razor; perhaps I am just no longer in the age group.

But if pain from chin pie was unwillingly endured, pain from smacking was positively demanded. When I read in Jessica Mitford's *Hons and Rebels* about their game of 'Hare, hure, hare, commencement', I instantly recognised a soul-mate. In their game the point was to endure unflinchingly the worst pain your partner could inflict by pinching your arm. Ours was more basic. With an air of 'Monster, do your worst!' we would upend our bottoms in a row and invite our uncle to hit them as hard as he possibly could—not that he ever put forth his full strength, of course—whereupon we would show him by our bland and debonair demeanour how admirably stoical we were. What a bunfight the psychologists would have over that now—or bumfight, perhaps.

Another of his tricks was to aver that we looked dirty and in need of a good cleaning. Then, when bedtime approached and we were preparing for our nightly wash, he would appear, a devilish leer on his face, with a carton of Vim and a big scrubbing brush in his hand. Great runnings, chasings and shriekings then took place. There was no doubt that he livened things up.

One night the grown-ups decided to stroll up to the pub at the village after their evening meal. They were not much in the habit of drinking beer, and half-a-pint each was enough for them, but they conceived the idea of pretending to return rolling drunk, as a joke for the children. But it was a joke that

33

misfired at least as far as I was concerned. When they came into view across the paddock staggering, supporting one another and singing snatches of raucous songs, I was scandalised. Acting outraged virtue with every fibre of my being, I rushed into the kitchen, and shouted importantly, 'They're all drunk—get the gun!'

One member of the family to whom every moment of the Penhallow holidays was an unmixed delight was our little white wire-haired fox terrier, Hervey. Although she was in fact a female she was always referred to as 'he'; he had a special accent of his own, which any member of the family could modulate into at the drop of a hat. All dogs, as far as we were concerned, spoke in this voice; cats had a different one. As our dogs and our cats were addressed exclusively in their own accents by everyone, they soon came to recognise them, and would look up and pay attention when they heard them.

Hervey loved the car. He often went round the practice with Thomas, my father, on his visits, sitting on the floor in front of the passenger seat. So he was well used to car travel, and did not mind the long day's drive from Yorkshire to South Wales; and luckily he was never car-sick.

We children, on the other hand, were just a bit inclined to be—or at least to feel—car-sick. The excitement alone was enough to bring on the feeling. The sorting of clothes, looking-out of bathing things, and packing of trunks that went on for days beforehand; the going to bed specially early with curtains drawn to keep out the light, on the eve of the journey; the setting-off, stiff-faced with sleep, and with a tight knot of excitement in your stomach, at half past five in the morning, all packed into the big, square Morris Isis. Knearsley revealed itself in a strange, fugitive beauty on those rare early mornings. The big mills still loomed black against the sky with their towering stacks, but as we slipped away down the steep main street, with everyone sleeping, the level sun struck motes of gold from the sandstone houses despite the overall dappling of soot; and the stone-tiled roofs stood up in stark, significant groupings against the pale early light. High above the clustering elm-trees of the churchyard reared the church tower, square, battlemented, uncompromisingly Victorian; and the weather-

34

cock on its top, glinting gold in the rising sun, pointed South-West—to the quarter of all delight.

It would still be early when we reached the foothills of the Pennines, and the smoke from Thomas's pipe would change from blue to brown as we breasted the thin skeins of cloud on their summits. 'Have your ears popped yet?' everybody kept asking everybody else. Hervey sat, impassive, at my mother's feet, by the passenger seat. Whether his ears popped or not we never knew.

At Buxton we made a long halt for breakfast. We always went to the same hotel, The Old Hall, where we could be sure of a good meal, and where we children could play for a while in the garden afterwards. We three looked forward year by year to this breakfast, which seemed to us to touch the giddiest heights of sophistication. To sit at a table in a great room full of other tables, with their silent guests—to be waited on by a God-like being in a boiled shirt and tail-coat—*at breakfast time!* —to be offered course after course, to select from the silvery ranks upon ranks of cutlery either side of one's plate—this was heaven. We enjoyed it down to the smallest detail, like the little balls of butter marked with a criss-cross pattern and garnished with parsley. We knew we must not address the other guests, but we could see the food that they were eating, and the richness and variety took our breath away. That man was having boiled eggs—ordinary enough, that was what we were most used to ourselves. But those two men were having kippers, and that woman was toying with a grapefruit. A fat man two tables away was having bacon and eggs *and* sausages *and* kidneys! And the little silver racks of toast brought to the table in a napkin! And the silver pots of coffee and hot milk and the dear little silver cream jugs!

When we resumed our journey, there were landmarks to look out for. One, which made me feel uncomfortable, was known as 'Libby's hedge'. In a moment of airy boasting the first year we came to Penhallow I had said, 'Do you see that hedge? I could jump that *easily!*' It was a wide overgrown hedge of hazels, about twelve feet high. Everybody had a little laugh at my jumping prowess every time we passed it after that, and I was always glad when it was behind us. Another landmark was

35

a burned-out house, a melancholy blackened shell that stared disconsolately through its blank ruined windows, about a hundred yards in from the road. Thomas and Elspeth liked it and often discussed what a pleasure it would be to rehabilitate it.

When we got into Wales we had to look out for the Sugar Loaf, recognisably conical, and we also waited for Builth Wells, where we stopped for lunch, and Pen y Bont, where we stopped for tea.

One of the best cures for car-sickness is singing, which necessarily leads to deep breathing. Many were the choruses of 'John Brown's Body' we ploughed through, followed by all the longest old favourites—'There's a Hole in my Bucket', 'Ten Green Bottles', 'I'll tell you one-oh', 'Nick-nack paddywack' and the rest of them. One of the songs was a special one, for Hervey, and we sang it several times every journey:

> 'Hurrah, hurrah, we've got the blessed pup,
> Hurrah, hurrah, the pup that cheers you up—
> How could we be happy if we hadn't got the pup?
> When we were marching to Gower!'

Hervey fitted admirably into the Penhallow way of life. He did not harass the cats, fight with the dogs or chase the poultry. By day he was out with my father, in the evening he lay by the grown-ups' feet as they played bridge and at night he slept in the car. He chased rabbits with enthusiasm but no success, and this led him to the nearest brush he ever had with accidental death.

We were sitting on the beach one morning, somewhere on the Penhallow side—probably by the Point, that charming little out-thrusting of barnacled rocks with a cave running deep underneath it—and Hervey had gone up onto the grassy cliffs above, in pursuit of his hobby. Suddenly a strange man came running from the next bay, and approached our group. 'Excuse me,' he said, 'but there's a little white dog fallen over the cliffs in the next bay, and I think it's yours.'

It was. Hervey lay on the stones at the foot of the cliff, deeply unconscious. Thomas felt for his pulse and found it small and thin. His breathing was slow and shallow. 'I'm afraid he's going to die,' said the man who had found him.

Just then a shadow fell across the little white body, and they all looked up. The new arrival was the Colonel, the landowner from whom the Evanses rented the Burrows. He had been shooting rabbits and had his double-barrelled shot-gun, broken for carrying, in the crook of his arm. 'God, what a pity,' he said, when the situation had been explained to him. His own black labrador nosed curiously at the still little creature, then, at a sharp command, went to sit obediently behind its master.

'He'll never recover from that,' said the Colonel positively. 'Better let me finish him off for you. Good job I've got the gun with me. Look what a height he must have come down!'

But Thomas had not yet given up hope. As far as he could tell, Hervey had sustained no injury beyond concussion, so, promising the Colonel that he would avail himself of his kind offer if it turned out to be necessary, he tenderly lifted the limp form and carried him up through the dunes to the farm. There he put him in the car, and waited. For the next few hours we all waited, and so did everybody on the farm.

And in due course Thomas's judgement was entirely vindicated. By mid-afternoon, Hervey raised his head in a dazed sort of way and looked about him. At four o'clock he climbed stiffly out of the car and drank some water. And when after dinner the grown-ups went out to walk along the sands, the tide being out, Hervey was able and willing to accompany them, to all appearances as good as new.

The Colonel too liked an after-dinner stroll. Purely by chance, they met him again, pacing along the sands with his black labrador, and when he saw Hervey he stood still in amazement.

'Well!' he kept saying. 'Well! I'm thunderstruck! I'm astonished! I should never have believed it!' A theme which he embroidered with subtle variations for several minutes.

As we children got a little older, we began to go with the grown-ups on some of their shorter walks. Going over the burrows to Rhossili beach was the first step. It wasn't very far—a mile and a half at the outside—but more than half of it was awkward walking, along narrow paths of dry sand running on ridges between great wind-sculptured dunes. We called it the Trackless Waste, and were always demanding rests while crossing it. Then, when we had finally prevailed upon everybody

37

to sit down for a few minutes, we would busy ourselves by collecting rabbits' droppings and threading them onto the spiky extremities of the tufts of marram grass. We called these productions Bigs Trees, and liked to picture the excited puzzlement of the many botanists and zoologists who, we were sure, infested the burrows, when they came across them.

It was hard work getting to Rhossili, but worth it when you arrived. For if Penhallow beach was domestic and the next one a miniature, Rhossili was majestic. *They* faced onto the comparatively quiet waters of the Estuary; Rhossili faced the Atlantic. Their waves could be rough and choppy, but the Rhossili waves after a south-westerly gale, were terrifying. The grown-ups liked to surf on them—not at the height of a storm, which would have been suicidal, but when things were calming down a bit. They did not have surf-boards—what went for surfing in those days was riding a wave on your belly, exciting enough for ordinary swimmers when the waves were nine feet high with a fetch of 2,000 miles.

We often went to Rhossili in blustery weather, drawn both by the magnificence of the surf and the shelter of the dunes. Nobody else would be there—in that great five-mile arc of golden sand and crashing white water, nobody but ourselves. We would scour the tide-line for driftwood, of which there was always plenty, and build a great fire in a dune which had its back to the prevailing wind. They were lovely, those driftwood fires, lavishly piled. Sea-blanched roots, tarred cork floats, broken, briny packing-cases, shaped and fashioned pieces of wood with copper nails in them, obviously parts of boats somehow smashed by the sea—the fuel was endless. And though the heart of the fire burned red and black, like any bonfire, the flames sprang magically coloured, brandy-blue, copper-green, royally purple, wonderfully transmuted by the strange alchemy of the sea. Potatoes, fresh dug from the Penhallow fields, would be buried in the sand beneath the fire. Then when we had bathed—oh! the fear and exultation of venturing into that white welter of water—we would run up the beach to warm towels, laid ready on big stones cunningly placed, and eat the hot potatoes as an epicurean first course to our sandwich lunch.

The trackless waste seemed twice as long and dreary on the

way home and we would gradually straggle off into a longer and longer line astern, calling plaintively 'Wait! Wait!' like seagulls, said our parents, or like distant bleating goats.

Penhallow usually had one or two fields of corn—one of oats, say, and one of barley—and being there for the whole of August, we were lucky enough to see them both reaped and carried.

Reaping day was an event; we would never have dreamed of going on a walk on that day. We wanted to be as near as possible to the thick of the action. Besides, we could help and to children it is a bigger bonus than many people realise to know that they are doing something really, undeniably useful.

All three horses had to be caught up and harnessed, for the reaper is one implement that takes a lot of horse-power. So the three big collars would be pulled off their pegs, twisted over the three gentle heads, the blinkered bridles put on, and then Prince, Duchess and Darling were led out, ready for the crowning day's work of the year.

Geoff would have been into the field the day before and scythed round it a couple of times to 'open' it; the corn he had cut was bound by hand into sheaves which leaned up against the hedgerow. You could look into the standing corn now, and see how the golden straw rose clean and strong from a tangle of green things round its root. There were flowers there, growing in the muted light at the bottom of the corn-forest; pink rest-harrow and creeping knot-weed; field convolvulus, gaily striped in pink and white; with here and there the yellow corn-marigold, or a vivid breadth of scarlet poppies.

Into all this beauty creaked and rattled that reaper and binder, huge, portentous, masterful. Mr. Evans, high on the driving seat, skilfully negotiated the three horses through the gateway, and wheeled them into alignment. Then 'Hup! Prince! Darling! Come on! Duchess!' and as they threw their weight into the collar the gears engaged, the machine moved forward with a shattering din. The long day's work had begun.

We loved to watch the binder at work. The big red sails in front flipped round so laconically, bending the corn onto the knife that killed it. The slain corn was carried away on an ever-moving canvas belt into the bowels of the machine to emerge,

39

miraculously, as sheaves beautifully knotted round with yellow hairy string. When the sheaf was ready, it was thrust off the back of the machine and fell, with a dry, rustling plop to the ground. And this was where we came in. We could help to stook. Even if, at first, we were not considered expert enough to ram the sheaf-butts hard down and lock their heads together, we could still carry sheaves to the stookers, and every saved step counts in a long day. And as we grew older we began to do the job properly, and properly it must be done, for oats must stand in the field quite a long time and may see some rough weather before they are safe in the stack. Oats, says the old country saw, must hear the church bells three times, which can be anything from just over two weeks to just under four, so obviously the stooks must be firmly set. The rows must be straight, too, for convenience in loading, and the noble simplicity of a well-set field of stooks is one of the greatest losses the landscape has suffered in my lifetime. 'Barbarous in beauty' is how Gerard Manley Hopkins describes stooks, but to me the primitiveness of their riches seems less obvious than their graciousness. Abundance, plenty, fruition are the words that are suggested to me by a stooked field of corn.

Other people had been reaping and carrying too, and the hedges that bounded the lane going to the village were skeined with snatches of corn plucked off passing loads by the long wands of the brambles. The blackberries were beginning to ripen, and as we went along to the post office to send our sepia views of Pool Bay or Brecyn Hill to the maids at home, we alternatively ate the luscious black fruits and the hard, hairy, strange-tasting grains.

Halfway along the upper lane you were joined by a little stream that ran prattling along at one side of the road. Gathering its forces as it went along, it was quite cressy and self-important by the time it reached the village. I loved its sotto voce tinkling in dry weather and its fuller gurgle after rain.

There were three shops in the village—the post office, Mrs. George's and the butcher's shop. Long, long ago, the story goes —many years before the time of which I write—there was a butcher in the village who had something of a reputation as a practical joker. One day, having just finished dismembering

40

a cow, his eye fell upon its udder, neatly detached, lying on the bench, and on the instant a plan was conceived. Picking up the udder he stuffed it into his trousers, with one long teat artistically arranged to simulate a careless, rather than a deliberate exposure. Then he tied on his blue and white butcher's apron, and betook himself to the bar of the local pub. It was high summer, and even in those days the bar was full of visitors. Having bought himself a pint, the butcher leaned back against the bar, and engaged some of them in conversation. They offered him a drink; he sank it quickly, and bought a round for them. Then he pretended to get a bit drunk. His voice became louder, attracting everyone's attention; and when, drinking too deeply at his next drink, he gave himself a moustache of creamy foam, he clumsily raised his apron to his lips to wipe it away. The visitors, embarrassed but worldly, tried to look as if they hadn't noticed anything amiss, but the landlord was scandalised. 'Hey! Pst! Look here!' he muttered, scarlet in the face, giving the swaying butcher a sharp dig in the ribs and an admonitory nod of the head towards the offending member. 'Wha's that?' asked the butcher, thickly. 'Ladies present! You're not decent,' hissed the landlord. 'Under your apron, man!' 'My apron? Whass amarrer with my apron?' queried the butcher loudly, gathering it to one side in his hand. When he saw what was revealed, he sorrowfully shook his head. 'That thing again!' he told the assembled company. 'It's always getting me into trouble!' with which, he drew his butcher's knife from his belt, and severed it at a blow. Then, to the accompaniment of a thin chorus of wailing screams and the thud of fainting women hitting the floor, he made one of the most dramatic exits that has ever been seen in that village.

I do not vouch for the truth of this story; I am only a channel. I pass it on as it was told to me.

Mrs. George's shop, though not the scene of such unusual incidents, was in other ways everything that a village shop should be. She sold all the things you couldn't do without at the seaside, like rock, postcards, shrimping nets, buckets and spades, and toy boats, spilling out of the door on fine days in gay profusion. Inside the shop was authentically small, dark and crowded. It had the proper smell, too, of a little country grocery; bacon, coffee, cheese and biscuits, laced with occasional strains of ambrosia when one of the big glass jars of humbugs or pear-drops was unscrewed. Mrs. George herself was small and whitehaired, and moved slowly round behind her tiny counter, murmuring to herself 'Elastic! Yes! I know I had some—black, it was—where did I see it now?' Only she could find things in the highly individual chaos of her shelves, and you had to give her time. But, like Ginger and Pickles, she usually had everything if you were prepared to wait. Thomas used to buy his tobacco there, and a daily paper, and there was always a great greeting ceremony, with much smiling and coming out from behind the counter and hand-shaking, on the first visit every year. 'The Doctor' was a great favourite.

That daily paper was the only contact with the outside world in the early days, but in 1938 a wireless made its appearance in the farm kitchen, and for days, it seemed, the grown-ups stood round it in attentive silence, heads bent, ears straining to catch the distant voice through the thunderous crackle of the atmospherics. We were aware, as we played our small games outside, round the duck-pond and rick-yard, of a doom-laden anxiety hanging over everything. What was it all about? Was it Munich—Chamberlain, with his pathetic negotiations and 'peace in our time'? No! Len Hutton was compiling his massive, record-breaking score against the Australians, and as good members of the Yorkshire C.C.C. my parents must hang on the commentator's every word.

Curiously enough, though, as it seemed to us, the atmosphere never really lightened. What was it that made the grown-ups talk so quietly and so seriously together now? Hutton had done it, surely—what was there to worry about now? I remember a few details about the slow slide into the war—Thomas, after we had gone home, sitting in his chair in the dining-room, the setting sun streaming over his shoulder, saying very gravely, 'There's not a ray of hope.' Elspeth, standing on the lawn in front of the house, talking to my father's partner, saying, 'Imagine seeing this very bit of sky black with planes.' Mr. Brady, a large, serious Irishman who came to build us an air-raid shelter, crushing beneath his heavy boots the sharp-smelling rowan-berries that the blackbirds dropped on him. We

42

boasted at school about our air-raid shelter, with its rubber-sealed door and its filter-pump to deal with ventilation during a gas-attack, but we never seemed to imagine ourselves actually using it. Christmas came and went. Everybody got fitted with a gas-mask; daffodils and crab-apples flowered; and then it was summer. And by then we all had something other than the war to worry about, because that summer we all got whooping-cough—badly.

Whooping-cough, if you must have it, is a good thing to get over in childhood. Phyllis, the dear aunt who used to be with us at Penhallow, got it just after the war, and I am sure she suffered with it even more than we did. Her cousin who lived in America wrote to her commiserating with her on 'your disgusting and humiliating complaint'. 'And nowhere in the letter,' said Phyllis to us, 'did she make any mention of what it was! Whatever must the censor think I've had?'

I was too young in August 1939 to bother about the humiliation, but disgusting it certainly was. By August we were supposed to be past the infectious stage, so we went to Penhallow as usual. I remember that journey as the only one in a lifetime that was pure misery. Anything might make me cough, and every time I coughed, I was sick. Not that there was much to be sick on—for once, breakfast at Buxton didn't tempt me, and I had to beat a hasty retreat from the dining-room at Builth Wells to hang, shamed and sweating, over a drain at the edge of the road. I was the worst but we were all being sick too often to stop the car every time, so Thomas provided us each with a deep, square, surgery-sized Elastoplast tin, and clutching these, we sat on the back seat of the car in a despondent row. Nurse, luckily for her, had left to marry an artist a year or two before, so was saved the squalor of having to share the back seat with us.

That year our party was augmented by yet another section of the family at Penhallow. My mother's sister, Aunty Mary, her husband, Uncle Jim, and their children, our cousins, Bruce and Judith, came to camp—seizing what looked like being the last chance for a holiday for some time—perhaps for ever; for it seemed certain, now, that war must come; and who, in 1939, would have dared to predict the outcome?

43

There was no early rising, no dewy milking, no riding of warm-backed cart-horses for me that year. Somehow or other the whooping-cough had temporarily affected my heart, and I had to lie about in the fresh air a good deal. Phyllis and George lent their canvas windshield, Aunty Mary provided a Lilo, and I was bedded out in a cosy little niche in the paddock, just by the garden wall. Feebly recumbent there one day, I was discovered by a strong detachment of geese and turkeys, who moved in pincer-wise with an unmistakably menacing mixture of gobbles and hisses. Possible heart damage seemed nothing compared to the imminent threat. Casting off my rugs, I leapt to my feet and dashed out through the narrowing gap, finding safety at last behind the back gate which I slammed in the very faces of my pursuers. Of course I got rebuked for rushing about but, as the alternative appeared to be being torn asunder, I felt that I must have chosen the better course.

One of the things you could watch, lying out of doors, when you tired of your book, was the wild ponies moving about on Brecyn Hill. Great tracts of land in Gower are preserved as commons; the roads wind, innocent of fences, over hundreds of acres of gorse, bracken, and sweet wild turf; and everywhere the pretty creatures abound. Penhallow did not own any ponies, which seemed a pity, but you could always see some up on the hill, and occasionally a herd would get down onto the beach, and pick its way up onto Penhallow land, grazing quietly in the paddock and round the buildings until the fancy took them to wander out onto the burrows and thence back to the common land again.

In many ways these ponies led a hard life, for most of them spent the whole year on the commons or the marshes, scratching for a living in the winter, and only hand-fed by their owners in the worst kind of snow. By spring the pregnant mares showed every rib, and you could see the poverty-streaks in their hind-quarters even through the teddy-bear thickness of their winter coats. There is no doubt that a higher plane of nutrition would have made them bigger—more useful, perhaps, by the same token, for their average height cannot have been much more than twelve hands. But they were well adapted to the environment, and somehow they survived and bred. Some

44

even grew up quite shapely, though others remained pathetic, stunted little runts—disparagingly referred to as 'Gower scrubbers' by the cognoscenti. They were often broken in for harness work, and were particularly popular with the cockle women of Penclawdd. They would drive down at low tide with their little flat carts to the cockle-beds in the Burry Estuary, equipped with rakes and sieves, and, some hours later, you would see the ponies straining back, the returning tide already sloshing round their fetlocks, and the carts burdened with several bulging sacks as well as with the fat cockle women.

But I liked best to see the ponies wild and free, in small herds or family groups, grazing the wide verges by some quiet farm, or drinking from some pretty rush-fringed pool on a green where the road divided. Each little group of mares would be attended by the young of the previous two or three years, from the fawn-like new foals (oh! how I would have liked to stroke them) to the two-year-olds, thin and nervous, whose burdock-matted forelocks streamed over their large, frightened eyes. By August the mares had picked up condition again after the rigours of the winter, and were fully established in their glossy summer coats. Full tails, slim legs, pretty heads—they made a charming picture as they moved, black, bay, chestnut, grey and dun, across the wild background of rock and furze.

There were donkeys too, roaming the commons, though never so many as the ponies. One day after breakfast when I was quite young, the grown-ups sought me out, smiling but portentous—all wearing their 'pleasant surprise' faces. 'Come and see what we've got for you, Libby!' they beamed. They conducted me to the cowshed hay-passage, from which you could look through into the stable. 'Look!' they whispered in hushed voices. I tiptoed into the gloom. There, in the velvet darkness of the stable, was a jenny donkey with a new foal. It couldn't have been more than two or three days old, and was about as large as a very big dog. The mother was a quiet old thing and, as she stood there so quietly, the baby was calm too, pressing up to her shaggy flank and looking curiously round at us with its astonishingly beautiful deep fringed violet eyes.

For a moment or two I thought that 'for you' meant what it said and that through some divine providence I had become the owner of this marvellous pair. But the grown-ups soon explained that the donkeys didn't really belong to us, that we could have a good look at them, but that then we must let them go again. So eventually we opened the stable door, and the mother and child walked calmly out, and grazed their way out by Rupert's house onto the bracken of the cliff-tops.

It turned out that the grown-ups, on their way back from an early morning bathe, had come across them grazing in the paddock, and had manoeuvred them into the stable so that I should not miss the chance of seeing them. I was off milking with Mrs. Evans at the time.

But it was ponies, rather than donkeys that I watched as I lay, slowly recovering, through the August of 1939. Uncle George and Aunty Phyllis finished their holiday and went back to London, but as August melted into September, the remaining grown-ups crowded, graver than ever, into the kitchen, round the faint, spluttering wireless.

And then, suddenly, it was upon us. The grown-ups heard Neville Chamberlain announce the fact that we were now at war. Then, seriously, but with resolution, they turned to the multifarious details of waging it, and life became submerged in a welter of arrangements. Uncle Jim had to get back to his London power-station; my father's partner, who was in the Territorials, had to join his unit immediately, so Thomas had to get straight home; and my mother, who was to do the partner's work 'for the duration' followed him in a day or two.

Aunty Mary was left at Penhallow to hold the fort and look after the three convalescent whoopers as well as her own children. Luckily we did not pass on our dread disease to Bruce, Judith or Marian; which was just as well, because although Richard and Gillian were now virtually better, I was still struggling. Night after night I would be sick, often in my sleep, and poor Aunty Mary would have to get up and clean me up, and give me fresh bedclothes. I don't remember feeling particularly ill, though I suppose I must have done. Mostly I remember the little treats and kindnesses that people arranged for me—a bright orange cup of golden syrup, brought by one of the campers for me to have on my porridge, with Priscilla's cream— a fireman's lift down to the beach when I wasn't allowed to walk (though I decided, ungratefully, as I hung head down, bumping, that if this was how fireman lifted, I should take care to avoid them)—a new pony book, bought by Mrs. Evans on her weekly trip to the local market town, and so on. Gradually I improved and, as autumn settled in at Penhallow, I was allowed to do more and more, until at last I was living a normal life again.

We had never experienced a country autumn before. Bruce and Judith's home was in London, ours near Leeds; everybody was expecting the Germans to launch a series of crippling air raids on our cities and everywhere parents were trying to get their children away to safety. Evacuation was being arranged as fast as the authorities could organise it—so, chance having deposited us in a place of rural safety, our parents decided that the best thing was for us to stay there, at least until such time as they could get us fixed up with places in some suitably remote boarding school.

Autumn showed Penhallow in a new and fascinating guise. For the first time we were there for the potato picking and grading, when the potatoes, damp and fresh from the sweet sandy loam, were shaken through riddles of varying sizes and put into store in different places, according to their ultimate destination. Ware potatoes, which Mrs. Evans sold in the market, were the money-spinners, but the ones we liked best were the tiny ones, the 'chats', which were put on one side to be used as feed for the pigs and geese. Like all children, we loved anything miniature, and in our minds' eyes Gillian and I saw these tiny potatoes as doll food. The skin came off them surprisingly easily, too, and I cleaned several with an industrious thumbnail before Marian happened to see me. 'You're going to have a terribly sore nail tomorrow, doing that, Libby!' she said. She was right.

My other effort at dolls' cookery was doomed to disappointment as well. Having listened many times to the story of King Alfred's culinary adventures, and having, more recently, read in *The Children of the New Forest* how Alice and Edith cooked cakes of barley meal on the hot stones in front of the fire, I was moved to emulation. True, I had no fire and no griddle, but the weather had turned hot again, and I heard Aunty Mary remark

47

to Mrs. Evans, 'You could fry an egg on the stones today!' Surely stones as hot as that could bake a few simple barley cakes? I looked around for some good flat ones, and fixed on some by the duckpond. They were certainly hot all right, in the burning blue and gold of a fine September day, but oh! the simplicity of a one-track mind. Obsessed by my idea, I made several trips to the barn, for a handful of barley meal from the barrel. Several times I kneaded it up with water, formed it into little flat cakes, and laid them on the grilling stones to 'cook'. Every time, when I went back to turn them over to do on the other side, they had disappeared. The only theory I could formulate then was that, lacking a binding agent, they had reverted to meal as they dried, and had been scattered by the wind, leaving no trace. The ducks, of course, could have enlightened me as to the fate of my little cakes, but instead they served their own interests by lurking cunningly in the rickyard until my back was turned, then sailing out in a determined flotilla and scoffing a whole baking in one fell swoop. They must have been quite sorry when in despair, I finally abandoned my experiments.

There were two duck-ponds at Penhallow. The one in the paddock was quite deep, and shelved up sharply to the green bank that bounded it. The other was at the back of the stables, and lay shallow, calm and placid, reflecting the whitewashed stone wall, and sometimes after heavy rain, extending a yard or two over the field, so that you could look down and see grass beneath its limpid waters. Here, with Marian, we constructed a marvellous system of canals, which we called Venice. There was no hard labour involved; beach spades chopped out the channels easily in the sandy, stone-free soil, and we played at it for weeks. It had all the pleasure of digging castles and moats on the beach, with the extra dimension of permanence. You could start afresh each day from where you left off, with no destructive tidal forces to reckon with, and the system of canals, intersections, leats, bridges and feeders grew and grew. 'Marian made boats for Venice' reads the only entry in Gillian's diary for the year 1939. Considering the material available to the diarist in that year, it seems remarkably parochial.

Every Friday, Mrs. Evans went to market, and, week by week,

we burdened her with our pocket money and our small commissions. We had phases for things. Celluloid teddies, about three inches high, from Woolworth's were all the rage for a few weeks (they went well in the boats in Venice)—then it was knitting. Mrs. Evans came across Richard one afternoon in the sitting-room, crouching doggedly over a skein of tangled wool.

'What are you doing, Richard?' she asked. 'Why don't you go out and play with the others?'

'No, I've got to stay in' he told her, raising a careworn countenance. 'I've got to finish my knitting.'

'Your knitting! What are you making, then?'

'A pistol holster . . .'

Potato-picking and cabbage-planting, as well as our watery games, were often interrupted by rough weather. The autumn gales at Penhallow were a new experience. We had once been there in a famous gale, when the gusts had been said to be reaching a hundred miles an hour; but all I could remember about that was that it had been frightening. We were older now—old enough to glory in the large rush of air, the low, hurrying clouds, and the tremendous smack! with which the sea hit the rocks beneath the cliffs, sending up fountains of spray fifty feet into the air. There were not many trees at Penhallow, and those that there were strained desperately landward, leaning away from the sea. You could easily see why when you had tasted those wild equinoctial gales.

It was blowing pretty briskly the day the threshing machine came to thresh out the two stacks of corn. A few farms in those days had fixed threshers in their barns, but most depended on a travelling equipage, and we were lucky to see one in action just before the invention of the combine harvester consigned them to limbo.

It arrived on the afternoon of the day before that fixed for the threshing—a two-piece affair, the traction engine with its great iron wheels trundling the long, tall box of the thresher behind it. Everybody is familiar with traction engines now from shows and steam rallies, but this one was in working dress. Instead of appearing in all the glory of gleaming brass and spotless paintwork, this one was black all over, as was its driver, and the only shine on either of them was the sheen of oil.

49

We heard it coming from almost half a mile away, and all gathered admiringly in the paddock to await the arrival, and watch the driver manoeuvring it into its working position. Advancing across the paddock with the stately deliberation of an elephant, the great steam-engine enveloped us in a shattering blanket of noise. Hens shrieked and fled through the rickyard; geese stretched out their necks with hisses of defiance until their nerve broke, when they turned and waddled away as fast as their fat bellies permitted; and the ducks, driven from their usual haunts, held a clamorous indignation meeting behind the stable, with much wagging of tails and passing of resolutions.

Clanking, hissing, and steaming, the monster backed and turned until it had deposited the thresher in just the right place. Then the pressure was let out of its boiler, the fire was allowed to die down in the firebox, and it was all carefully sheeted up for the night.

It was an early start the next morning, and work was well under way by the time we appeared on the scene. Refreshed by copious draughts of water from the duckpond, the black monster roared and clanked, and we stood, awe-stricken, transfixed by its marvellous smooth power. The pistons and couplings slid to and fro in their appointed tracks with such an irresistible force; the great driving belt trembled and hummed as it impelled the spinning wheels, and a huge racket arose from the bowels of the threshing machine which seized the sheaves and ripped them apart, showering straw forth from one orifice, and clean, bright grain from another. Snatches of steam, sparks from the fire, and chaff or 'cavings' blew wildly up into the low grey sky, and the human attendants (including several neighbours who had come to help) darted here, there and everywhere, like busy ants.

Some passed the sheaves from the stack to the feeder, who cut the strings, and gave the corn to the machine. One fixed new sacks onto the grain outlet, and tottered, with the sixteen-stone full ones, up the outside steps to the barn loft. Others built the threshed straw into neat stacks, or cleared away the mounting heaps of cavings. The driver tended his fire, oiled things, and twiddled screws that controlled the pressure in the boiler. It was all, as Chaucer would have said 'en bustle and rout', and rest was very welcome when the last trickle of corn had run into the sack, and the last forkful of straw had been built firmly into the peak of the big stack. The silence was doubly precious, seeping back as the giant clanked and rumbled away to its next farm, by contrast with the frantic noise and activity of the day. Tomorrow, Harry would take Prince with the flat cart down to the dunes for a load of marram grass and the new, long straw stack would be thatched and made weatherproof, fit and ready for the winter which was now almost upon us.

And it was not only winter which was looking over our shoulders. Our parents had always intended us to go to boarding-school in Wales; the coming of the war simply advanced this plan by two or three years. Places were hastily arranged for Gillian and me at Dr. Williams' School, Dolgelley, while Richard's school evacuated all the boys of his age to temporary accommodation in Fairbourne only a few miles from Dolgelley. In many ways it was all rather convenient.

As a matter of interest, the shattering bombardment of Leeds and Bradford that everyone so fearfully expected never took place. Why, I don't know. Both were up to their eyes in war production, but a very mere scatter of bombs—one of which destroyed my grandfather's vicarage—was all they ever got. One theory I have heard is that the course of the River Wharfe rather resembles that of the River Aire, and that instead of following up the latter and finding the two cities, the German navigators kept getting the former, where the best that they could do was to knock hell out of Gordale Scar. It may be true.

Fear of the event, however, even though it never materialised, led to our being shipped off to the safe area of Dolgelley. It was all very strange at first, and in the daunting jungle of boarding-school life, I was cut off, for a time, from anything to do with farms or farming. But all comes to her who waits, and eventually I got my foot into another farm door—this time of the lovely and gracious Bryn Farm, about two miles from Dolgelley.

PART II

THE BRYN

Jane Austen's Catherine Morland would have liked Bryn Farm; she would have found it romantic. For, like Northanger, it was built round an abbey. The monks' dormitories, and what you might call the service areas of the abbey, had been adapted to make the house and the dairy-cum-granary complex that faced it across the little flower garden. Tiny leaded-paned windows and immensely thick stone walls testified to the antiquity of the place, and a Victorian fireplace with hob and side boiler in the kitchen only partly filled up the vast chimney-place, with its high-backed settle forming a warm, draught-free corner for weary men to sit in.

A fine double avenue of limes lined the stone road that swept up to the farm, and at the far side of the home field were the remains of five or six noble walnut trees that dated from before the reformation.

The cowshed and stable, with rickyard behind, were about fifty yards away from the house, tucked against the beginning of the rising ground. And in between improbably towered the Abbey Church, gauntly beautiful. The Ministry of Works was technically responsible for its upkeep, and they had constructed a neat wire netting fence around it, dignified by a tall beech hedge; but the real work of maintenance was performed by a handful of Welsh mountain sheep who lived among the ruins, and kept the turf like velvet. For drinking they used the little tinkling stream, channelled in stone, which ran through the precinct, and for shelter they lay in the ruined apse. You could always see some of them there, cudding quietly where the altar had stood and the choir had chanted, while now only the wind sang, tossing the yellow wall-flowers on the ruined sill of the great east window.

Monks have always been noted for their skill in choosing good sites for their abbeys, and the builders of the abbey at Bryn were no exceptions. Away to the south, the midday sun looks over the nobly sprawling range of Cader Idris, and, westering, sinks over the long glinting reaches of the Mawddach estuary. Salmon run up the river to spawn in their due season; standing on the old packhorse bridge, you can see them in the clear brown water. The swirls and eddies round the piers of the bridge have scooped out deep pools on the seaward side, and the long, shadowy shapes lie there, half seen, with fins flickering against the current. Woods of oak and sweet chestnut clothe the steep sides of the river valley, and the rocky bumps of Diffwys and Precipice Walk shelter the farm from the north and east. Ninety acres of enclosed land with extra grazing on the marshes down by the estuary and an open sheepwalk up above the Precipice form quite a large farm by Welsh standards, and it was run as a well-farmed traditional holding, with a dairy herd of Welsh Blacks providing the backbone of the income.

It was through Gilly that I got to know Bryn. Gilly arrived as a new girl in my form at the beginning of the second year, and life for me lit up instantly, as if curtains had been swept aside to let in floods of vivid sunlight. I was ten, and she was twelve, and I had never met anybody like her. She was tall for her age, and extraordinarily fearless, dark-browed with grey eyes that looked at you very squarely from a brown face, and straight, thick, silvery-fair hair that fell to her shoulders and was cut in a fringe over her brow. When she grew up she was beautiful, but it was her personality, not her looks, that struck me so forcibly as a child. She had spent a year or two at the famous Bedales School before coming to Dr. Williams'; perhaps it was this that had shaped her to such originality and confidence; perhaps it was innate in her. At any rate, she seemed to have about twice as much vitality as anybody else, and we immediately became 'best friends'.

We spent all our time together, breeding rabbits (Dutch ones) and talking about horses. We affected toughness and the out-door life, and we used to have long, competitive cold baths in the early morning where you took it in turns to get in, and lay submerged in the icy water counting aloud, and trying to stay

53

in longer than the other person had. The glow that followed the brisk towelling-down when you emerged was augmented by a trot round the extensive school grounds. 'Who are these hearty people?' languid prefects would ask each other as we tumbled, rosy and thoroughly awake, into the dining-room for breakfast. We were labelled as eccentric but harmless; in general nobody minded, as long as they weren't required to do the same.

Sometimes the school grounds seemed too small to contain us, and we would break bounds, squirming along, Indian-fashion, behind all the natural cover, until we reached the beautiful seclusion of a marshy lake about two fields away, known to everybody as the Mangrove Swamp. We never got out for the sake of perpetrating any crime—rather the opposite, indeed; we found a cast sheep one day and, by restoring it to an upright position, probably saved its life. It wasn't for the sake of adventure that we got out. It was for freedom—freedom, and a kind of outdoor reality that was very distant from the rather prissy and old-maidish standards of school. When the farmer who owned the field next to the Mangrove Swamp ploughed it, we had to walk on it, to smell the fresh-turned earth, and to examine and handle the two-furrow plough that he had left at one end of the field. We both intended to become farmers even then.

Gilly's family owned a caravan which lived permanently at Bryn Farm, and her parents used to stay in it whenever they were able to visit the school to take their daughters out for exeats. In the kindness of their hearts, they offered the use of it to my parents too, for holidays, and the offer was gratefully accepted. As it was wartime, and Thomas and Elspeth were running the practice between them, they could of course only go away one at a time, and usually only for a week each at that; but even a week was a marvellous unwinder, in such a remote and beautiful place. Everybody needed a bit of rest and refreshment as the war dragged its slow and often desperate way along.

So, one day, at the end of July 1943, Gillian and I, instead of getting on the going-home train with all the rest of the girls ('No more marg., full of hairs, scraped up from the kitchen

54

stairs—what've you got in your sandwiches?'), walked a mile and a half in the other direction, and joined our mother and Richard at the caravan for our first proper stay at Bryn Farm.

The caravan (the only one on the farm then) was parked by itself in the field with the venerable walnut trees. Huge and grey, they lined the stone wall between our field and the next, and the caravan was right beside one of them. Only one or two still bore leaves; most were dead, and reduced by time to branchless trunks of gnarled silver. But they were august and noble, and we were glad that they were preserved and protected by the Thomases almost like heirlooms.

The Thomases themselves were an old Welsh family who had farmed The Bryn for many generations. They still kept to the custom of using 'ap' which means 'son of' in their name; thus Will was 'William ap Gareth' and his son would be 'Robert ap William', or whatever; but Robert ap William was still far in the future at the time of which I write, for Will was a bachelor of twenty-five and lived at home with his mother and his older sister, his father having died some years previously.

I was mad with joy to find myself on a farm again, and instantly familiarised myself with the layout—the long, dim whitewashed cowshed, scrupulously clean and swallow-haunted —the cobble-floored stable, with its corn-bins and rough home-made hazel pegs for the harness knocked in between the un-plastered stones—the pig-cote, where two inquisitive, white-eyelashed young gilts rushed out to investigate any noise—the races and pens and dipping-baths for the sheep—and, nearer to the farm, the orchard, with three beehives under its sunny wall. Since Will was the farmer, and *ipso facto* the prime mover in all the farm action, I instantly attached myself to him, and trotted after him wherever he went like a little dog.

It had been a catchy year for weather, and the hay at Bryn was still waiting to be cut. The climate of North Wales is a few weeks later than ours, and to be haymaking at the end of July was not so very unusual. But there was a fair pressure of work to be done, and everyone expected to work long hours to accomplish it. Especially Will. Will showed me which was his window on the front of the farmhouse, and told me to come and wake him up as early as I liked. 'Come and throw stones at my

55

window, and when I stick my head out, shout "get up, you lazy lout",' he said. So I took him at his word.

In the middle of the caravan field there was a little movable henhouse, in which the poultry were shut up for the night to keep them safe from the foxes. But although they were closed in, they could see the dawn through the window, and no sooner had the east begun to pale behind the mountain than the cockerels would crow. Lying in my bunk, scarcely thirty yards away from them, I would awaken, and joy would instantly pour in a scalding flood through my whole being at the thought of another farm day beginning. Slinking into my clothes, I tried to creep out of the caravan without waking my mother, but she slept so lightly that I never managed it. She said it didn't matter, though—she was able to get back to sleep again after I had gone.

They were so magical, those summer mornings before the sunrise, that their essence has stayed with me ever since, and even now, the sound of a cock crowing awakes a little reminiscent glow in my heart. It would still be almost dark when Will emerged, yawning, from the house, pulling his cap on the side of his head, and tightening up his belt—a broad leather one, studded with brass hearts and diamonds, that I much admired. A pale remaining moon augmented the tentative light from the east as we picked our way through a dew-soaked monochrome world to fetch the cows in for morning milking. It would not yet be four o'clock when we had them in the cowshed, all tied up in their places ready to begin.

The cowshed, which was stone-built, must have been at least two hundred years old. Deep embrasures in the two-foot-thick walls held useful things like bottles of black drench and pots of udder salve; the milking stools stood upside down in a row on a shelf cut into the wall's thickness. In front of the cows, a wooden partition divided them from the hay passage, whose floor still held about a foot of last year's hay, springy and fragant. The twenty or so Welsh Black cows, and Meirion, the bull, stood quietly waiting as the milkers carried in the shining pails from the dairy, picked up their stools, and addressed themselves to their task.

Everybody milked at The Bryn, and everybody but me was

an expert. I was provided with a bucket, a stool and a quiet old cow, and I pushed my head into her shining black flank and worked away, happy to find that the technique acquired at Penhallow had not deserted me, even if my muscles were still not all they might have been. Milking is like riding a bicycle— you never forget how, once you have got the trick of it.

Sometimes I would get my first cow finished in time to get on to another one, sometimes not. Will usually finished off the last two or three while his mother and sister carried the fragrant, foaming pails to the dairy for straining, cooling and bottling. Most of the milk was sold retail in the neighbourhood. Going back to the caravan for breakfast, I carried two or three bottles of it for us, and my mother waxed lyrical over its quality. Not only was it deeply creamy—albeit not yellow, like Jersey milk —it was also, she said, the best milk for keeping that she had ever come across in her life. There were no gas refrigerators in those days; the caravan larder was a metal gauze safe, nailed onto the trunk of the dead walnut tree, and shaded by a luxuriant elderberry bush, but in spite of the heat of the perfect July weather, the milk never seemed to go sour. It remained sweet for two or three days—a tribute to the spotless hygiene of Mrs. Thomas's dairy.

While I tagged round after Will doing the milking, and, after breakfast, the milk round, certain other jobs on the farm were done by Cedric, the farm-hand. He was a morose, dark-haired man on the wrong side of fifty, who looked at the world with a gloomy, sallow countenance, and chewed tobacco. I sometimes wondered if he might be better-tempered if he wore less, because even when loading hay or corn beneath a burning August sun, he wore clothes fit for an Arctic winter. A thick Welsh flannel shirt, collarless, was open at the neck to reveal a Chilprufe vest, whose long sleeves peeped out where the shirt-sleeves were rolled back. On the evidence of the clothes-line at washdays it seemed that he wore long Chilprufe pants as well, under his thick corduroy trousers. Over all, a waistcoat was tightly buttoned. 'It helps to soak up the sweat,' he would say, when I impertinently asked him why he wore so much wool in summer. I pointed out that if he took some of it off there wouldn't be so much sweat to soak up, but he only flung me

57

a morose glance and ejected a spit of clear brown tobacco juice not too far away from my feet before slowly turning to re-apply himself to his work.

While we were milking he would have gone down to the river-meadows, caught up the horses, and fed them. After turning the cows out, he would shovel up the muck and wash out the cowshed. It was all timed nicely so that the horses had had time to eat and digest their feed, and were ready for harnessing when Will came back from the milk round.

There were three horses, Duke, Luce and Clwyd—but Clwyd was temporarily out of action. One of the other horses had kicked him, laming him with a nasty deep cut, just where the front legs join the chest. The vet had given Will some lotion to put on the wound, but the big bay gelding kept licking it off, so he had to stay in the stable, tied up rather tightly. Presumably his rope was loosened at night so that he could lie down.

The work, then, fell on the other two, Duke and Luce. Duke was my favourite, a sixteen-hand dark brown gelding, with a moustache, a white stripe down his nose, and the expression of gentle, suffering goodness that many cart-horses have. Luce, a black mare, was a good hand smaller, and more lightly built, but she was still more of a cart-horse than a cob. Both were hard and willing workers, and they managed to match their strides without any apparent inconvenience in spite of the difference in their heights.

The two of them were harnessed to the old land-driven mower, and off we went, rattling deafeningly up the steep, stony lane, to the first of the hayfields, to start the haymaking. Round and round the field we went, the horses pulling gallantly, Will on the high metal seat of the machine, and me plodding behind. Will thought I was daft to waste so much labour, and constantly told me so. 'Why don't you go and sit by the hedge, Libby?' he would ask, when he paused to 'breathe' the horses. (The thunderous clamour of the machine when it was working made any kind of conversation impossible.) 'You can see just as well from there.' But he was wrong; I couldn't. I had to be there, where the action was, as close as I could get. I wanted to drink it all in, to be part of it—to have my ears deafened with the machine's clatter while the mingled scents of sweating

58

horses and fresh-cut grass assailed my nostrils, and my eyes reeled from the incessant flashing to and fro of the bright knife, flickering away down there at the root of the sorrels and the tall red clovers. Sitting demurely in the hedgerow, I would have been a mere spectator, a visitor, a nothing. And as for fatigue, I didn't know what it was in those days. So I tailed the machine all morning and, before we left the field at lunch-time, pulled from the cut swathe a bunch of the sweetest, most honey-scented red clovers as a present for the convalescent Clwyd. He received it with approval, as Duke and Luce clattered into their stalls, to feed and rest for an hour in the stable's cool dimness.

In the afternoon, Luce was harnessed to the tedder, and plodded to and fro while its busy little rotating forks fluffed the hay out behind her. And now there was a chance for me to be useful, and do some real work. We had brought a bundle of pitchforks and wooden hayrakes into the field with us, and while Will rode up and down on his clanking chariot, the rest of us turned and tossed any particularly thick or tangled sections of the crop, and raked the outermost swathe out of the hedge, where it would never have dried properly. You felt it, after an hour or two of that work—in your shoulders, your arms your back; in the soreness of your hands, sliding con-tinually over the smooth ash of the fork-handle, and in your skin, which glowed and burned with the day-long exposure to the sun and wind. But pride prevented me from referring to it, or slowing my pace of work. It was a relief, nevertheless, when Mrs. Thomas appeared in the field gateway with a basket of sandwiches and a can of lemonade and we all downed tools for an interval of rest and refreshment. Luce, too, was glad to stop for a while, and stood in the shade, nodding away the flies and snatching mouthfuls of sweet grass from the hedgerow.

There was an etiquette, I soon discovered, in the matter of the lemonade can. We drank in turns from the lid, and you were supposed to leave the last drop, which you ceremoniously swilled round the lid and tipped out onto the ground before you handed it on to the next person. The fact that the outer side still bore, unwiped, the impress of your lower lip, apparently didn't matter. A sop had been cast to the Goddess of Hygiene and that was the important thing. Or could it have been the last remnant of an older custom, a libation to the fruitful earth, its true meaning now forgotten? It didn't matter in practice. Not being first in line, I was able to copy the motions correctly, and I was aware of a sense of social pitfalls circumvented. I was always anxious to behave correctly in those days, and to be accepted by those I admired.

Tall bracken grew out of the hedgebank, stretching up to meet the arching sprays of the dog-roses and the hazels. Little brown-and-orange Gatekeeper butterflies flitted here and there, or perched, wings momentarily spread, on the lichened, sun-warmed stone gatepost. I could have sat for an hour, watching the tiny shadows of the grass-blades slowly working round to the east, but work called; there was another hour's tossing and tedding before evening milking, and another milk-round, de-livering pints and quarts round the cottages in the little secret lanes of the village in the bat-flitting twilight.

Then we would gather in the farmhouse kitchen for supper, and eat prodigious quantities of home-made bread, farm butter, newly churned, and blackcurrant jam. The fire burned in the big black fireplace; the kettle, hanging on the pot-crane, whis-pered sibilantly; and the oil lamp, hanging over the table, spread its benign, honey-coloured glow over the tired workers, relaxing in the warmth and peace.

But it was not all work and no play at The Bryn, even in the height of the haymaking. One evening Will said something to his sister in Welsh, and with an affirmative nod, she went to the kitchen corner and fetched out her harp. I had never even noticed it before, in its canvas case in the shadows, but now it emerged, gilded and beautiful, and soon it was tuned, and her fingers were rippling over the strings, letting its lovely liquid notes fill the room. She played tunes I knew, and tunes I didn't know; she played 'Merch Megan', 'Bugailio'r Gweneth Gwyn' and 'Mari fach'; and now I recognised the notes of that most famous of Welsh airs, 'The Ash Grove', and heard Will, sitting there on the oak settle, chime in with a penillion.

The penillion is a peculiarly Welsh musical form. The harpist plays the air and, part of the way through it, the singer comes in. He sings contrapuntally, weaving his melodic line around that of the harpist, but making it different, and, in particular,

60

not exactly following his time. Both parts, however, must end simultaneously, on the keynote. Penillion are really supposed to be improvised, but most performers learn famous ones that have been written down. The effect of them, when properly done, is quite sophisticated.

At thirteen I was old enough to be well aware that this spontaneous display of a culture going back, perhaps, thousands of years, was a rare treat, and my head was full of the romance of it as I walked back down the fragrant, rustling avenue of limes, to the caravan field and bed.

As well as its ninety-odd acres of enclosed land, The Bryn had substantial grazing rights on the open mountain above Precipice Walk, and here Will kept his flock of several hundred Welsh Mountain sheep. I suppose everybody knows by now of the bond that keeps a sheep on an unfenced mountain—that knowledge, imprinting, almost, of territory, handed on from each ewe to her lambs which keeps them on their home patch more securely than any fence ever devised. Generations of Bryn sheep had grazed those particular heathery hills and rocky cwms, and there they stayed, and there Will had to go to shepherd them.

For this work, he kept a pony, and in the spring of 1943 he had just acquired a new one. It lived in the caravan field, and I thought it was the most beautiful creature I had ever set eyes on. It was young—a three-year-old gelding—and stood about 13.2 hands. In colour it was the brightest of chestnuts, with two white socks and a white stripe, and its mane and tail were flaxen.

When he had first arrived at the farm the pony had pined and refused to eat, so they had christened him Gandhi after another eminent faster. He was a splendid pony but he had just one fault—he was difficult to catch. I tried to make friends with him, offering him bread and carrots on my outstretched palm, but he only snorted warily and kept his distance, grazing twenty feet away, with one dark eye turned back to keep me under constant observation. I didn't want to harass the poor creature so, after a few attempts, I left him alone, and thus, paradoxically, won his confidence. I was waiting for breakfast one morning, and I had come out of the caravan to

61

put some rubbish in the dust-bin. Gandhi was grazing close by, and, setting my empty bucket down, I gazed at him dreamily. Suddenly, to my surprise, he raised his head, and walked hesitatingly towards me. He paused—then as I made no movement, he came right up to me and pushed his nose towards me. I made no attempt to touch him, and he examined me carefully, smelling me all over and touching here and there with his soft, bristly lips. Then he wandered away. Flattered and amazed, I rushed into the caravan and 'borrowed' a thick slice of bread, which I sprinkled with salt. Moving slowly up to the pony, I offered him a morsel, and this time he accepted it with every appearance of satisfaction. Soon he allowed me to scratch his copper neck, where the cream mane flopped over, and to pull his pretty ears; and, after that, I could go up to him any time. This was convenient for Will; he could tell me when he was going to need the pony, and I could catch it up and put it in the stable ready for him, thus saving a lot of time and frustration.

When Will rode Gandhi up the mountain after the sheep, three dogs ran at the pony's heels. Toss, the fourth, was too old to go now; stiff and half blind, he drowsed the hours away in a sunny corner near the lime avenue, where the beehives stood against the orchard wall. But Moss was there, and Bright, and Fly. Moss and Fly were conventional enough border collies— pretty creatures, with flat, silky coats, and long noses. Bright, though, was quite unusual. He had thrown back in type to the old-fashioned Welsh sheepdog, largely displaced in the nineteenth century by the fashionable Border collie, and his general style was woolly rather than silky. His coat was a sort of tweedy mixture of browns and greys, with white paws and linings, and his head was wide and deep-skulled, rather like the head of an Old English bobtail. But whereas the bobtail wears its hair over its eyes, Bright's were always visible, and very appropriate to his name, for they were of the most luminous, intelligent hazel. Everybody who came to the farm wanted to buy Bright, but he was a good dog at his work, and Will would never part with him.

Some shepherding jobs needed the sheep brought down to the farm, and it was wonderful to see the three dogs managing the flock with the minimum of human assistance on these occasions. Dipping for scab was compulsory in those days (as it has become alas! again) and Will brought the sheep down into one of the grass fields to be ready for our early start on the next day. We didn't need the pony to fetch them in to the holding pen then; Richard and Gillian came along up the steep green fields to help gather them, and to manoeuvre them through the rocky knolls, crowned with young oak trees, into the farm lane, from which they could not escape. 'For we are like sheep,' said Will to Richard, almost pityingly, as the slender creatures hustled along, bleating anxiously and casting back fearful glances from their yellow eyes.

The Welsh Mountain sheep is as custom-built for its range as the wild pony, and hard necessity has turned it into something rather beautiful. It is small compared with a lowland sheep, and its fleece is harsh, to shed the rain which falls on the mountains at the rate of a hundred inches per annum, or more. The tail is left long for protection, unlike the docked stump of the lowland sheep, and the legs are slender, active and deerlike. The finely-chiselled face is framed by a pair of large, mobile white plush ears, and the eyes are golden. The pupil in a sheep's eye is horizontal, which gives it a curiously inscrutable air. They look as if they can see right through you, to mountain horizons far away, on the rim of the world.

What I particularly liked about them when I was thirteen was that they were not too big for me to handle. Active and strong they certainly were, but when you locked your fingers firmly in the wool of their backs and set your weight back, it was no contest; you could drag your ewe, struggling vainly, to the dipping-bath, where Will heaved her in, Cedric ducked her head under, and a fat policeman in his shirtsleeves supervised the whole proceeding, and took note of the number going through the bath. All was bustle and action, with a constant discord of harsh bleatings, the grunts and swearings of the catchers, and the recurring splash! of the sheep, thrown into the deep disinfectant dip. Working among the dry sheep, my nostrils were full of their characteristic smell; it was on my hands and clothes, ground into the very being of me, but I didn't mind—I liked it. I still like the smell of sheep very much indeed. In fact, nearly all clean farm animals smell nice; the exceptions are poultry, and bulls' breath.

At the other end of the dip the acrid smell of the disinfectant crowded out all other scents, and the drenched sheep stood streaming in the holding pen, shaking their heads furiously to clear their ears and eyes—their expression showing quite clearly that you had confirmed their worst anticipations on the subject of man's inhumanity to sheep. But they soon got over it, and when they were dry again Will took them back to their mountain pastures where they resumed their unfettered existence.

At the end of a week my family went home, but I was to stay for a further fortnight at the caravan, with Gilly and her mother. There was one night when I was unaccompanied. I would have been happy enough to sleep alone in the caravan—I could always lock the door, I told my mother, and anyway, who was there to harm me, there in the deep country? But she wouldn't have it, and as there was no room for me in the farmhouse, arrangements were made for me to spend the night in the village.

The people who took me in were a Jewish couple, refugees from Hitler's persecution, whom Gilly's family had befriended. They had had to leave Germany with nothing, and I do not know what they lived on, but there they were in a pretty little cottage in the village, and I quite enjoyed the cosmopolitan air of the household as a contrast to my rude open-air life. Mr. Casera was a violinist, and when, after supper, I had been conducted to my bed in a room with sea-green brocade curtains, he began to play. It was a Bach partita, I think—I meant to listen—but I was full of fresh air and food, and work well done —and I drifted off to sleep on a confused thought of the richness of life—Bach, violins, sea-green curtains, and Will singing in the kitchen.

The Thomases were fond of Gilly as the Evanses were fond of us, and the very air of the farm next day breathed a happy anticipation of her coming. One of their uncles, Uncle Ewey, was spending a week or two with them at the farm, and he kept us all informed of her progress. He worked as a guard on the railway, and knew all the times of the appropriate trains. 'She'll be at Reading now,' he would say, pulling out his watch from his waistcoat pocket, or, even more impressively: 'In exactly six and a quarter minutes, she'll be pulling into Ruabon!'

And then she was there, with her wide, friendly smile, and her casual confidence in the essential *manageability* of the world. Most people went along with her, and enjoyed the vitality, the fun, and the genuine originality of her personality. But not everybody. Not, for instance, the biology mistress at school, who received in answer to a question on an exam paper 'describe the structure and seed dispersal methods of the dandelion' a brief answer which read 'dandelions are used for telling the time if you haven't got a watch' illustrated by a lively drawing, in her rather Thurberesque style, with the caption 'One o'clock! Two o'clock!'

The school drew in its lips and was not amused by this sort of thing, but Gilly didn't care. Her family's bent was artistic and musical rather than academic, though her father was an accomplished linguist, and, like George Borrow, had taught himself to speak good colloquial Welsh.

As always, in her company, I found my horizons broadening. She showed me a much better bathing pool than the one we had been using, higher up the river; and every day we swam and floated in the limpid, peat-brown water. We rode Gandhi too, in the flat fields by the river, and constructed little jumps for him of logs and brushwood. Then, when the sun was climbing up the sky, we would turn him back into the field, and borrow Bright to take him up the mountain to 'our' farm.

It was a lucky discovery, this farm that we called ours. It was empty, and almost derelict, with hedges that had degenerated into gappy lines of trees, and patches of bracken appearing in the pastures, but we thought it was perfect. We imagined what it would be like to live there—when we discovered that you could get into the house by a loose window at the back, we even went to the lengths of choosing our bedrooms. I must say that certain details of our ménage had to be glossed over because imagination would not stretch that far—in other words, our husbands. We both intended to be married, but the practical difficulties of finding husbands who would be willing to be farmers, and, in addition, to share a farm, were so obvious that we just had to gloss over them, and elide them, so to speak, from our dream-plans.

When we set out to Mynnydd Du (as our farm was called) the first thing to do was to cross the river. A charming bridge with three or four arches and pointed piers carries the road across, but we spurned this in our youthful singularity; we had to walk across the river bed. Further to point our difference from the rest of mankind, we never took our sandals off for this ritual. Accompanied by the fragrance of crushed river mint, we would lower ourselves down the bank, and into the knee-deep water. Clear and brown, like china tea, it swirled round our knees, plucking hard at our feet as we balanced our way over the slippery stones. Refraction made our legs look all wrong, as if they were bent where they entered the water; it was quite a relief to pull them out, straight and reliable as ever, on the farther side. Water gouted out of our sandals as we scrambled up the bank, but the leather became so porous that they were dry before we were half-way across the field that now lay between us and the village. The borrowed dog at our heels— Bright or Fly—shook itself mightily, showering us with a cooling spray—and, slipping under the fence, we drifted through the village as unobtrusive as shadows.

It was only a hundred yards to the gate that led to the steep, grass-grown track of our property. Wide fields sloped gently down on our left as we climbed; thick woods clothed the steep hill that fell away to a stream on the right. In a moment we were screened by the thick-leafed boughs from the sight of anybody in the village; now, we felt the place was truly ours.

Up at the house, you reached the upper limit of the enclosed land. Behind you rose the open mountain, fold upon fold, austerely beautiful in its covering of grass, bracken and heather. Once the fields had been separated from the rough grazing by a great stone wall, but in the pre-war years of depression, this had fallen into decay. There were gaps you could have driven a team through, and the mountain sheep ranged the low pastures as freely as the high ones.

The farm buildings were also in a sorry state, with dereliction everywhere. Patches of sky showed in the roof of the tiny cowshed, and one wall of the pig-cote had collapsed outwards, undermined by the nettles which triumphantly invaded the pigs' little courtyard. Half the roof was gone from the open-ended cart shed, too, and more would have fallen if it had not been for the great cloud of ivy that surrounded it and to some extent provided it with support. But the three walls were sound, and this cart shed provided us with a focus for our main game. For our prime reason for coming up every day to Mynnydd Du was that we wanted to play with the sheep.

We were well aware of what the grown-up world would have had to say on this subject; we took pains never to be discovered. It was for this reason that we traversed the village with such discretion, and welcomed the shelter of the first friendly belt of trees. It was not that we ever did the sheep any harm or upset them in any way. At that time of year there were no young lambs with them. There was nothing to go wrong really, but we still felt guilty. After all, they were not our sheep. We didn't even know whose they were. But our urge to work the dog and handle the sheep was stronger than our guilty feelings, and all they served to do was to make us extra careful not to be found out. I suppose young people always spend their time testing their capabilities by acting out the situations that they expect to meet in adult life, and this, we felt, was very like the real thing. We were proud to be able to manage it alone.

We took it in turns to work the dog. We had watched Will using him, and noted the calls and whistles that sent him hither and thither, or dropped him, a panting statue, on the grass. Sending him away with a wide sweep of the arm, we would collect a bunch of, say, twenty-five animals, and work them into the barn. There we would pen them behind an old hurdle we found leaning against the wall (doubtless left there for the same purpose by their legitimate owner) and survey them with pride as they milled to and fro, bleating.

There wasn't much we could do in the way of pretend work with them once we'd got them penned; we would catch a few specified individuals, and turn them up, sitting them on their tails between our knees as if we were going to trim their feet, but obviously, we couldn't actually do anything to them. We found an old, old pair of shears hanging on a nail in the wall, and experimented a bit in their use, but without success. Perhaps they were too rusty and blunt—perhaps it was our technique that was at fault. At any rate, we never succeeded in detaching a single fibre from any of our victims. And when we had tried, and hung the shears back on the nail, there was nothing else to do but to pull back the hurdle and let our captives stream away into the sunlight.

After handling the sheep, we always went further up the mountain, to where a small lake lay in a fold of the ground, its rippling waters reflecting the ever-changing sky. Here we would swim, often naked, to wash off the strong give-away smell of having handled sheep. It remained on our clothes, of course, but our clothes were always horsy, cowy and doggy, so presumably nobody noticed that they were a bit sheepy as well. At any rate, nobody ever said anything.

The lake was not very big, but the middle was very deep—local tradition said it was bottomless. It was also supposed to contain a monster which would come up and 'get' you if you tried to swim across, from one side to the other. Not being very brave, I swam only within my depth, putting an experimental toe down every now and again to reassure myself that the coarse, glittering white sand of the shelving bottom was still there. Gilly was bolder, and swam further out. Her older sister was not to be deterred by any silly folk-lore, and she swam right across, and lived to tell the tale. But that was on another occasion.

When we had had our swim, failing always to persuade the dog to come in with us, we would lie on the grass in the sun until we were dry, and then run home, all wet hair and innocence, for lunch at the caravan.

The afternoons were devoted to rather more serious work. The hay, tedded and turned in the fine hot weather, was ready to cart, and had to be raked together and put into cocks ready.

It is curious to think that a whole generation has grown up to whom a hay-cock is nothing more than a thing in a nursery rhyme—as detached from reality as little boy blue and his horn. Haycocks, like corn-stooks, epitomise the farming I used to love, that has gone for ever. The very word carries a warmth of memory about it, a suggestion of sunny days and hard work

68

done right and in due order. The famous Haycock Inn, with its evocative sign, still has this effect on me, though I have only once entered its portals. I was there for lunch in my youth and I quite unintentionally embarrassed my youngest aunt. She and I both needing to visit the 'Ladies', she conducted me thither. Our way led through the residents' lounge, and twelve or fourteen of the residents were there, stretched out in the armchairs dozing, and enjoying their after-lunch coffee. Captivated by their torpor, I paused for a good look at them, and, as I was hustled away, asked in clear ringing tones, 'Arno, are those men all drunkens?'

Putting up the hay into cocks at Bryn Farm that summer of 1943 was better than any May-games with somebody else's sheep. It was the men, mostly, who actually made the haycocks. We women swept the hay up to them with hayrakes, whose wooden teeth were repaired as an evening job in the winter, with dowels of peeled hazel cut from the farm's own hedges. 'There was plenty sweating in those days, but plenty laughing too,' as my neighbour's old father told me; and we did sweat too, down in those flat fields by the river, where the hay was full of meadowsweet and wild mint, and tall hedges of willows and hazels cut off the cooling breezes. But one of the points about handwork is that you can go at your own speed and, if you know you will have to keep going for a long time, you pace yourself, and don't try to move too big a mountain of hay at one time with your rake. There were plenty of us, too, for one or two neighbours came in to help; and in the event we got all the hay cocked without having to work ourselves sick.

With the weather continuing fine, the next job was to carry the hay into the barns, and here again Gilly and I were lucky for it must have been one of the last opportunities to see this being done on that most traditional of Welsh vehicles, the gambo. It was a kind of sled, really, pulled by a single horse in chain harness; having no wheels it was stable on steep fields and over rugged ground, but the increased friction with the ground meant that the horse could only manage quite a small load. Clwyd was better now, and was back at work, so the three horses all participated in the carting, and, each with its own gambo, ran a steady shuttle service between the field and the barn. Gilly and I were allowed to help pitch on to the gambos, but were not skilled enough to build the loads, which was quite a difficult job. One of the men would do that, but we didn't mind; we had our own learning to do, and thoroughly enjoyed our increasing strength and skill in skewering a haycock cleanly, and depositing it conveniently, just where the loader wanted it put.

It was fun, too, taking the horses out to pasture in the evenings. Their grazing was by the river on the far side of the road, so we took them over the flat fields bordering the farm drive, and every evening we had a race. Bareback, with only a halter, we thundered along like the Norman cavalry, the horses quite willing to shake a leg in spite of the day's work behind them. Generally I rode Duke and Gilly rode Luce—our favourites—leaving Clwyd for Will; but sometimes we changed about, and we were disgusted to find that Will always won, whichever horse he rode. We would pull up from our reckless progress before we reached the road, and, leading our horses carefully across, take them through the gate and slip the halters over their heads. Then we would stand and watch them as they wandered away to graze, before we turned to walk back to our various beds through a twilight tremulous with owl calls.

It was while we were still busy getting the hay in that the corn came ripe, and the tractor with the reaper and binder came from the 'Warag' to cut it. Every farm had to grow what corn it could in those wartime years, and Will had two fields, one of barley and one of oats. Many farmers had not been growing corn in pre-war years, and as they lacked the specialised reaping tackle they were able to use the facilities offered by the War Agricultural Committee or 'Warag' against just this eventuality. So Duke, Luce and Clwyd were spared the labour of pulling a binder, and the Warag's old Fordson, travelling with its own driver, did the job instead. It took him a day to cut each field, and we were in behind him as soon as possible, getting it stooked. We finished the oatfield on the day it was cut, before milking, but the barley field was bigger. 'We'll go up after supper,' said Will, 'after we turn the horses out, and have another go at it. We'll finish it in an hour, surely.' So after supper up we all went.

It was a high rounded field, the sort they call a 'breast' in this part of Wales, and when you were working in it you could look right down the flat light-reflecting reaches of the estuary. The sun had set before we started our work, but for a time the field was illumined by the afterglow and, even when that faded, the pale shine of straw and stubble gleamed luminous against the darkening sky. Presently the moon came up, preternaturally enormous over the shoulder of the hill, and our stooks cast pale, sharp shadows as we slapped the butts down on the ground and locked the rustling heads together.

I was enjoying the work, repeating to myself the lines:

'And by the moon, the reaper weary
Piling sheaves in uplands airy,'

and thinking how divine a providence it was that the work and the poetry gave and took from each other such a compound interest of excellence, when a sudden violent commotion directly behind me nearly made me jump out of my skin. It was Cedric, the staid Cedric, rolling on the ground in the ruin of an eight-sheaf stook and shouting like a maniac. For a second or two I thought he must have had a fit, and in horror I was just about to look at Will to see what his reaction was. But, with a final wriggle and a desperate squeak, something tore itself loose from Cedric's grasp and rushed away into the night, all big ears and long back legs. It was a hare! Lying doggo in its form, it had obviously left it too late to run away, and if Cedric had been ten years younger there is no doubt that jugged hare would have figured on the farm menu. But his reactions were a shade too slow, and though he flung himself full length on the ground with an abandon that would have done credit to a slip fielder, 'puss' just managed to slip through his fingers. Gilly and I were secretly glad, but it would have bitterly offended him for us to say so. Normally morose and taciturn, he was lifted quite out of himself by this unusual adventure, and re-counted to us over and over again just how the hare had been lying, what thoughts had flashed through his mind when he had first seen it, and what he had said when he saw it disappearing over the horizon.

As the corn was in fields which were flatter than the

71

hayfields, it was carried to the rickyard, when the time came, on a flat waggon rather than on a gambo, and this circumstance led to a narrow escape for me, which showed up very clearly how all too easily accidents can happen in farming.

We had loaded up the cart with sheaves, and the load was on its way out of the field, with Duke in the shafts and Luce in the traces. That particular field, and those adjacent to it, had stone walls, and as it happened, the track out of it ran between two of these for a distance of about ten yards outside the gateway, like a short section of narrow lane, before widening out again into another field. Will was walking alongside Luce, guiding her through the gateway with a hand on her bridle, and I was a yard or two behind him, level with Duke. As we came into the narrow bit, I decided for some reason to stand still and let the load pass me, which might very well have been the last decision I ever took on this earth. For what I did not realise was that the load was coming through the gate at a slight angle, and as it came level with me it seized me between itself and the wall in an ever-tightening grip. Useless to shout—no noise I could make would reach Will's ears over the clatter of eight hooves, and the thunder of four iron-shod tyres over the stone of the track. So as the horses plodded on, I was pinched tighter and tighter, and rolled round and round like an oat in a mill. Panic images of death rushed to my mind, but luckily before the pressures reached rib-cracking point we reached the end of the narrow bit, and it spewed me out, to collapse on the grass beside the track, more dead than alive.

I know I am foolish and in some ways cowardly, but I have all my life been hyper-sensitive to a rebuke. Once, when I was six, I approached a horse in a field from behind and touched it on the flank. It kicked me on the head, knocking me unconscious for a few minutes and leaving an absolutely unconcealable lump as big as an egg on my right temple. I remember then that I hung around that field miserably for over an hour, afraid to go home and acknowledge to Aunty Mary, with whom I was staying, what a damned fool I had been. And now, rolling around on the grass gasping for breath after my crushing, I was fiercely determined not to tell anyone about it, and spare myself at least the humiliation of the acknowledgement. So

72

when Will, glancing back and seeing me sitting there, shouted, 'Tired, Libby?' I nodded brightly, and fetched up the best grimace of a smile that I could muster. As soon as I could get to my feet, I skulked behind the load and quickly felt myself all over for damage. And I was lucky; it was nothing like as bad as it might have been. The back of my left hand was badly scraped and bleeding—it bears a small scar to this day—and my right shoulder felt as if it had been torn from its socket, but when I experimentally moved it, I found I could put my arm through all its normal range of movement, though it hurt. And as it was lunch time, I had a chance to sit down unnoticed once we got down to the farm until all feelings of faintness and sagging at the knees had passed. My side and shoulder stiffened up overnight and I had a terrible job to put my shirt on in the morning, but pride was a sufficient spur, and I managed it somehow.

Concealment was rendered easier by the fact that my holiday was now virtually at an end and I had to get back to Yorkshire. Conveniently enough, Mr. and Mrs. Casera, the kind couple who had taken me in for the night, were going north, and it was arranged that I should travel most of the way with them, leaving them at the last change, Manchester, and completing the journey alone.

I am ashamed now to acknowledge that it was a sore trial to me to travel with them. I was ashamed of myself then, too, which added to the inner irritation. The trouble was that they behaved so obtrusively humbly. They hung back at every doorway and carriage entrance; they squeezed themselves apologetically into the worst seats, darting cowed-animal glances at all the other occupants of the carriage; when they produced a packet of sandwiches and began to eat, I could scarcely bear the cringing way they bent over the paper and mumbled the food, looking up this way and that from under their eyelids like dogs that expect to be kicked. I was proud, and protected, and I was terribly afraid that everybody else might think they were my parents.

I was perfectly well aware that they must have acquired this awful humility during the years in Hitler's Germany when they were persecuted as Jews, but my youthful inexperience stiffened

73

me with embarrassment as the result. I leaned back in my seat, looked out of the window, and refused a sandwich.

My conscience still troubles me over this odious display of bad manners. I wish I had had the social experience—or perhaps, simply, the warmth of human compassion—to draw them out, perhaps to set them into conversation with other people in the carriage, to relax the atmosphere a bit. But I didn't know how to do it, and we parted at Manchester in the end with expressions from me of polite thanks but without any real cordiality.

Life in the countries that came under Hitler's sway certainly left its mark on many people. Years later, Gilly went to work at a riding stable run by two Polish refugees, father and son, who had somehow managed to get out of that country after the war. 'At the end of the first course at lunch, on the first day,' she told me, 'they said to me "You are finished, yes?" and when I said "Yes", they plunged onto my plate like a couple of vultures and gobbled up all the little bits and gristle and fat I'd left on the edge of it!'

My connection with Bryn farm might very well have come to an end at this juncture, because Gilly's parents, feeling that the discipline of Dr. Williams' was too restrictive, removed their daughters to the more liberal atmosphere of Beltane School. But to my great joy, my mother managed to make an arrangement with the headmistress that I should be allowed to come along to the farm every Saturday afternoon, and ride, instead of playing games.

So, although I never actually stayed on the farm again, I became a regular visitor, and saw it in all its phases of work, and in all seasons of the year. Saturday after Saturday I stumped along the road, saddle on my shoulder, noticing all the little familiar details. Dog-violets and wild strawberry flowers by the roadside in the early part of the summer term gave way to the little scarlet fruit in July, or, if I came the back way, avoiding the main road, I could pick wild raspberries, and ponder over the pink-freckled stonecrop on the walls. The leaves of the sweet-chestnut trees were clear yellow in autumn, drifting down to hide the prickly-hedgehog nut cases, from which I would

74

save a pocketful of nuts to roast in the fire on hair-washing nights. Damp November evenings, with the light fading, would smell of wet moss and oak-bark; and towards Christmas I might be lucky enough to see the towering mountains white with snow, glinting in the sun that warmed the scarlet bravery of the big hollies.

Even on days when the rain sheeted down and riding was out of the question, I would try to sneak away unobserved, getting out the back way so that nobody should stop me; for what did a wetting matter, compared with the chance of a couple of hours' freedom, and perhaps the chance of participating in some delightful farm job? There were lots of useful jobs that could be done in wet weather. Will might be crushing oats in the mill, or sawing logs with the circular saw, or pointing fencing-posts with a few well-placed blows of a machete. Or there might be a new animal to see and admire. Over the years, the original horses were all sold, and more came in their place. Duke, Luce and Clwyd were replaced by a pair of greys—Daisy, who was a fairly nondescript mare, and a most beautiful iron-grey two-year-old gelding. He was called Colonel when he arrived, but it must have been an acting rank only. In the interests of euphony, Will demoted him to Major. When you are working horses, you keep up a kind of running fire of admonitions, encouragements, commands, and ratings, liberally interspersed with their names, and 'Major' seemed to go more easily into this than 'Colonel'. The two greys made an impressive plough-team, but in the onward sweep of progress they were eventually replaced by a Fordson tractor.

Gandhi, too, was sold, and in his place Will bought a dark bay cob, which, coming from the home of all the best cobs, Cardigan, was duly christened Cardi. Cardi was exceedingly quiet at first—almost dull—but, perhaps because he hadn't enough to do, he became more and more tricky, and ended up an absolute devil. He was far from easy to catch, for one thing, and even when you managed to get him into a corner of the field the battle was by no means over. Quite often he would whip round as two or three of you closed in on him, and charge his way out to freedom, threatening you with bared yellow teeth and blazing eyes. I really think he would have trampled

75

on anyone foolhardy enough to stand in front of him. He was a determined character.

Nor were your troubles over once you had caught him, saddled him, and mounted. He became 'nappy', in other words, unwilling to go where you wanted him to, and always trying to swing round and be disputatious. When you compelled him with heels and stick, he was inclined to rear, and occasionally he liked to seize the bit between his teeth and indulge in a good bolt. I can't say I much enjoyed riding him; I got to the stage of putting him into a standing martingale and a twisted snaffle before venturing out in the end; with this rather severe bit I did at least feel I had some modicum of control. And to those who are wondering if the rearing had something to do with the twisted snaffle, I will say, no, he started rearing first, and besides, I was well aware of the severity of the bit, and used it with delicacy.

Cardi caused me acute embarrassment at school on one occasion. Deciding to do some jumping, I had constructed a little course of a log and a tiny brush-jump, arranged between two little ditches. He jumped the first ditch well enough, and scrambled through rather than over the brush; but when we arrived at the log, he suddenly decided to say no, stuck his forelegs into the ground and stopped. I went on, and arrived some way up his neck, on his hogged mane—but before I could wriggle back into the saddle, the perverse creature decided to jump after all, and bucked over with a horrible arching heave of his back. Arriving on the far side, he stopped again, abruptly, and, chucking up his head, caught me full in the eye with his poll. A city that is set on a hill cannot be hid, and nor can a black eye that would have done credit to Joe Louis. I was terribly afraid that the headmistress would say that it was too dangerous for me to go riding, or something of the sort; but though she looked at me rather quizzically, she did not ask any questions. My own contemporaries both asked questions and offered uninvited comments, but that did not matter.

After a while Cardi was sold, to my relief, and was replaced by a liver chestnut called Fan. She was a nice enough animal, and I enjoyed riding her for several years, until I left school.

One curious phenomenon about the riding is perhaps worth

76

recording. One track I used to ride along went up along part of a well-known route called 'Precipice Walk'. It was an old road, partly grassy and partly stony, and on its way it passed through some abandoned copper-workings. No grass grew there; the copper ore had poisoned the earth all around, and the ruined buildings on either side of the track had a sad, desolate air. But the nastiest thing was the stream. It ran parallel with the track and, where it went through the workings it had been channelled in a bed of granite masonry. And, through this, it flowed quickly along in total silence. I hated the place, and always rode past it as fast as I could—a matter not easy, for every horse I ever took there had to have a battle before passing it, and accelerated away afterwards as if the devil was after it.

I had never mentioned this to anybody, so I was rather impressed, when, years later, talking with my father about immanent evil, he mentioned that same stream as having the most positive atmosphere of evil that he had ever experienced. But the place where he felt it was not at the workings, but about 200 yards further up.

Sometimes I had a companion on my rides, a girl from my school, somewhat younger than me, whose parents lived nearby. I enjoyed going out with her and her little roan pony for several reasons; for one thing, it is always more entertaining jogging along in company than alone; and, for another, I occasionally went back to her house for tea after the ride, which I enjoyed immensely. The tea itself was no small part of the pleasure, of course. Boarding school food, notoriously bad, degenerated to little more than subsistence level during the war years. But, even more than that, there was the delight of being in an ordinary domestic situation for an hour or two, in the cheerful comfort of a pleasant lived-in house, with two little sisters sharing the rug before the big log fire with a couple of superannuated gundogs, and a cat or two. It was a house full of history, too—family history. It had been the dower house of the family for hundreds of years, and every room was full of treasures, the accumulation of things that generations of people had thought worth keeping about the place. Rummaging in her chest-of-drawers for some horse pictures she wanted to show me, Susan would casually push aside a silver-mounted inkwell, made of a horse's hoof. That was a relic of a favourite charger that had belonged to a great-great-uncle. Or a fox's mask mounted on a wooden shield, commemorating some notable hunt, would catch my eye, hung on the wall in the small passage leading to the bathroom. I was aware of the weight of social history in the place, and felt sure that wonderfully interesting boxes of letters and things lay, like buried treasure, in the dusty attics.

The ancestral estate of this family was only a mile or two away, and Susan and I often rode up there. Our object was not the house itself, but the deer park, in which we were allowed to ride. I don't know how big the park was—the hilliness of the terrain made it difficult to judge its extent—but its grassy tracks, overhung here and there by gnarled oak trees, provided us with delightful riding territory. Even better was one circuit of about a quarter of a mile known as the racehorse gallops which had been developed for that purpose by some sporting ancestor. They might not have won the admiration of a Newmarket trainer, but we thought they were wonderful, and urged our sweating, grass-fed ponies along them at the best speed they were willing to offer.

It was a beautiful place, that deer park, with its sheep-nibbled green tracks cleaving through the shoulder-high bracken, and usually at some stage of our ride we were lucky enough to see some deer, couching under the oak-trees, or bounding through the bracken with antlers laid back over their shoulders. In summer, cuckoos cuckooed, green woodpeckers laughed, and woodpigeons cooed among the shadowy branches. Drifts of foxgloves testified to the acidity of the soil, and occasional outcroppings of bilberries promised a feast to the patient picker. Lady's bedstraw grew there too, abundantly. You could make a dye out of it, our art mistress averred—a yellow dye; but, as the years went fleeting past, that was one of the many things I always meant to try, and never got around to . . .

PART III

FOXWOOD

Everything comes to an end at last; and, long though my school-days had seemed, they eventually drew to a close. I was still determined to be a farmer, and the most promising step in that direction seemed to be to go to our local university, Leeds, and read for a degree in Agriculture.

I put my name down for the course, and learned that, before starting on the academic bit, I must complete a year's practical work on a suitably modern, well-run farm. 'Look in the small ads in the *Farmer and Stockbreeder*' suggested the Dean. 'There are plenty of vacancies there. You should get fixed up at a good place without any trouble'.

In the event, I was lucky, and got the job at the first farm I applied to, a 500-acre mixed holding in the prettily-named village of Rook's Moat, in Shropshire. My mother came with me for my interview, and fixed me up with digs in a most elegant Georgian guest-house down near the church, about ten minutes' walk away from the farm. 'You don't want to start in the middle of winter,' she said sensibly enough. 'Stay at home until April, and then you can start in the nice spring weather.'

I thought of her words as I sat on the bus from Shrewsbury to Rook's Moat. Sleet splattering against the windows obscured the rolling, well-wooded countryside that I tried to watch as the bus hurried along. I felt excited and nervous. How would I make out, in this, my first foray into the adult world? It came to my mind that it was All Fools' Day; I hoped it might not be an omen.

But when the bus came to its terminus in Rook's Moat, a tiny incident cheered me up. I noticed that somebody had left a package on the seat in front of me, and I drew the driver's attention to it. 'I wonder who left that?' he said. 'And what is it, anyway?' With which he opened the bag to disclose that most basic property of all Northern comedians, a fine black pudding, lying coiled in smug ebony symmetry. It seemed to me like a friendly, reassuring clap on the shoulder—what could go very wrong, really, in a world full of black puddings, of jolly bathos, and of sturdy common sense?

'Don't come up till after breakfast on the first day,' they had told me, when we had made the arrangements for my starting work. So I waited till nine o'clock before I walked up the hill to the farm, stiffly self-conscious in brand-new boots, brand-new dungarees, brand-new everything except my old leather jacket which I clutched round myself for what reassurance it could give. It was evident that nobody had much idea of what to do with me at first. Everybody was busy, bustling about their accustomed tasks, and I hung around, feeling shy and superfluous, until old Mr. Driver, the father-figure, arrived on the scene, and found me a job. Leading me to the space at the end of the cowshed where rations were mixed and feed stored, he pointed to a great heap of tangled, rusty wires. 'Those are the wires off the hay-bales we've been feeding to the cows this winter,' he said. 'You untangle them and put 'em in neat hanks, and perhaps we'll be able to find another use for them later.' He knew, and I knew, and I knew that he knew that I knew that he was talking nonsense; but anything was better than standing around 'with my two hands the one length', so I fell to with a will at my fatuous task, and when those wires were finally thrown away, they went to the rubbish-heap in neat hanks, rather than in a tangled mess . . .

Old Mr. Driver was technically retired, though still very active, and it was his son, Martin, who ran the farm and to whom I actually considered myself apprenticed. He must have been in his thirties at the time—a pleasant-looking, kindly young man who wore tweed jackets and cavalry twill trousers and looked the very model of a successful gentleman farmer. But what I liked about him was that he worked as well. He was nearly always there at milking-time, in a faded, patched old milking-coat, among the cows, or cartoning the milk in the spotless dairy. He was a good horseman, too, and a good 'boss'. He ran the farm on thoroughly modern lines, and I thought

80

myself lucky to have got into such a good situation for my year of pupilship.

When Martin arrived on the farm after breakfast, my instruction began in earnest. He introduced me properly to Jean, the landgirl, and she took me under her wing, and showed me how to dismantle, wash, and sterilize the milking machines, usually referred to as 'the units'.

A lot of my work during the next year was done in Jean's company, so it was lucky for me that she was such an exceedingly nice girl. She was older than me, nineteen to my seventeen, a good deal bigger, a friendly, pretty girl, with a fine sense of fun, and an astonishing capacity for hard work. For looks, you might have picked her out of the whole land army to represent a kind of idealised figure of a land girl. She was brown and rosy, with brilliant blue eyes and wavy brown hair, and deep dimples appeared in her cheeks whenever she was smiling, which was usually. Strong and buxom, she looked good in the sensible, workaday uniform of the Land Army, and like a classic Christian, I suppose she pitied my simplicity.

When we had finished the units, and packed them in the big sterilizer to be steamed, we went up to clean the cowshed. As it was April, the cows were out grazing during the day; they had been turned out at night, too, but the weather had become so cold and sleety that they had had to be brought in again—'The first time,' said Martin, 'that I've ever had to do that in all my farming experience.'

The men had done a quick shovel-up of the night's muck before the milking began, but several barrow-loads had accumulated since then, and the first job for Jean and me was to clear it away. We loaded it into the wheelbarrow and wheeled it out behind the cowshed, where we shovelled it again, out of the barrow, into a curious vehicle known as the muck-cart. Viewed from the side this was U-shaped in section; a horse drew it over the fields and, at a suitable moment, its conductor operated a lever which caused it to tilt over backwards, slopping the muck gradually onto the land. Sometimes, when we were very lucky, the man who drove the horse would drive him slowly through the cowshed so that we could shovel the muck in directly, and save ourselves a job.

There had been two carthorses on the farm for some years, Punch and Tommy, but on the very eve of my arrival, something very curious happened. Tommy, grazing in the field as usual, suddenly began to gallop. Running, inexplicably, like a mad thing, he ran head-first into a large tree, and broke his neck. 'Broke a blood-vessel, sure!' said all the old men; but post mortems don't pay any bills, and Tommy's body was hauled to the hunt kennels uninvestigated.

That left Punch as the only working horse on the farm, and a very good horse he was. As his name indicated, he was a Suffolk, a clean-legged liver chestnut, unbeatable at a dead pull. He was honest and willing; he had, indeed, only one fault. As a result, presumably, of some childhood trauma, he was terrified of brushwood, and if he heard the crackling and snapping of twigs, he was off, and there was no holding him. Watkins, who drove him, was well aware of this foible, and took care to avoid anything that might upset him. 'But you dew have to look out,' he would say, 'when they be trimmin' those hedges. If he was to step into one o'they piles o'brushin's, there's no saying where he might stop. Shrewsbury, happen!'

When we had disposed of the muck, with or without benefit of Punch, Jean and I washed the cowshed. Water from the roof ran off into a storage system, so we were able to use that, and lavishly. In the winter only the rear parts of the standings were washed, so that the cows had a dry bed to lie on. In consequence, the fronts of the stalls gradually clarted up with trodden straw and spilled food, which welded itself onto the concrete like a second skin. Jean began to attack this as soon as the cows were turned out to grass, and it was her pride to have it all down to bed-rock concrete inside a week. I was happy to do as she did, and together we soaked, scraped and scrubbed, gaining a little bit every morning. I still value such little but genuine satisfactions—it is better, surely, to feel a little pang of triumph as a well-aimed bucket of water suddenly carries away a recalcitrant plate of muck than to plod through the day's tasks feeling sorry for yourself because everything is dull and boring? Jean and I preened ourselves on our beautiful clean cowshed, and when the floor was perfect, we started on the mangers, and cleaned all the windows. The mangers were glazed

82

earthenware, and the cows used to dribble into them until you could scoop out the spit by the pint. Little bits of hay falling down into this would accumulate in the corners in a nasty, black, evil-smelling mess, which it was very satisfying to move. Interestingly enough, our cows at Penllwynplan never dribbled into their mangers in this way. Maybe the food we gave them was less appetising!

Certainly the cows at the farm were lucky in this respect, and I often used to think I wouldn't have minded tucking into some of their food myself. Martin mixed it himself from various 'straights', and although it was extra work, it was cheaper, and in many ways more satisfying than the ready made cake that we all use today.

The ingredients were all so nice, for one thing. The foundation of the mix was usually brewer's grains, the crushed kernels of sprouted barley from which the malt has been leached, which, as a brewery by-product, was pretty cheap in those days. A lorry from the brewery backed through the big double doors at the end of the cowshed near my heap of untangled wires, and tipped it into a big heap on the floor, where it waited, fresh, damp, and smelling pleasantly of beer.

I can't remember the exact proportions of the things we used to add to the brewer's grains—it varied, I suppose, with the fluctuating prices of the various ingredients. But everything was attractive. There was steamed flaked maize, bright yellow and sweetly scented, like animals' cornflakes, and weatings, a fine grade of bran from the flour-mills. Often we added rolled barley or oats from the farm's own granaries, and a bag or two of fish-meal or meat-and-bone-meal would go in at the end to provide a suitable proportion of protein. Martin turned and turned the heap with a broad shovel, and the dampness of the brewer's grains slaked the dust of the drier ingredients. The smell changed, too, as the mix amalgamated, reminding me of one of the first cookery lessons I had ever had. My mother (who was busy with some other job) was telling me how to make force-meat balls, and I was fascinated by the rich variations in scent as I assembled the ingredients one by one. 'Fresh breadcrumbs —a pinch of thyme—get some parsley from the garden and chop it, a good handful, that's right—now a couple of grinds

83

of black pepper and some salt—and a good grating of lemon peel—now pour on that melted butter, it must be ready by now . . . ' and as the hot butter sizzled into the other ingredients, a blended savour arose so mystic and so wonderful that I felt the act of eating the things had become almost superfluous. Similarly with the cows' mix; one felt that the acme of perfection had been reached when the blending was completed, and the heap stood, fresh and appetising, on the floor. The cows, though, were victims of no such sentimental illusions, and waited, drooling uncontrollably, until they received their rations, which were chalked as a figure denoting so many scoopfulls, on the silver milking-machine airline over each stall.

The cowman was a little, white-haired, acerbic gnome of a man called Gosling, addressed as 'Gos' but referred to in his absence, inevitably, as Goblin. He was not a countryman by birth, but a cockney. Some freakish tide of chance had deposited him in the heart of rural England, and there he stayed; but he sounded different from the other farm workers even though the years had rubbed the sharp twang off his London accent. He was as used to farm pupils as to cows, having seen many of both come and go, and having showed me how to wash and forestrip a cow and clap the unit on her, he told me to get on with it. I did feel anxious, I recall, about stooping down so close to those big, unfamiliar back legs but he reassured me, impatiently, 'They don't seem to kick me, do they? Why should they kick you, then? Get on and do it, girl, and I guarantee at the end of a week you won't be giving it a thought'—a prophecy which, of course, turned out to be right. For the first couple of milkings he did let me shirk the 'funny' ones who could not be relied on to stand still, but as soon as I acquired any kind of competence he insisted, very properly, that I take my place in the routine and do them as they fell to my share, without fear or favour. So of course I did. One or two of them had to be restrained with a tight girdle of rope, but only one was a real 'performer'. She was a cow called Grace, who stood third up on the right-hand side, and if not restrained, she would have kicked the milker and the milking machine to kingdom come. A rope round her middle was inadequate for her; she had to have her hocks fastened together with a special leather strap and, like a fool, she always

84

allowed you to put it on without any fuss at all, clearly not connecting it with the frustration of her kicking attempts later on in the proceedings. Jean was Grace's salvation in the end; after a long course of patience, gentleness and perseverance, she got her so calmed down that she didn't need the strap, but accepted the inevitability of the milking machine as placidly as any of the other cows.

It was a good place to be, Foxwood Farm, in the prosperous year of 1947. Foxwood we called it, for that was the home farm; but the family also owned Blacklees, the next property, and there was 100 acres of reclaimed land rented far away. The farm was over 500 acres at the time, and was farmed in accordance with the most modern principles. A dairy herd of about sixty Ayrshires provided milk for a retail round—any surplus was sent to the creamery. There were pigs too—Wessex saddlebacks, but the buildings where they were housed were some way from the main farm, and I never had anything to do with them. I was warned on the first day to stay well away from any sow with piglets I might see in the fields. 'Praaper savage they be,' said the farm men. 'She could bite through your leg as easy as she'll bite through this mangle, see!' So I did not court the company of pigs and, as it happened, there was plenty to fill my day without them.

There were the sheep, for one thing. There were over 500 ewes on Foxwood and Blacklees, and the shepherd was always complaining gently that it was too much for one man to look after. He was a real Shropshire man, steady and ruddy, with dark eyebrows, and keen grey eyes. I got the surprise of my life when, about four months after my arrival, I first saw him without a cap on, a condition which revealed a mop of golden hair. 'Why, Bill, you're *fair!*' I exclaimed, much to the entertainment of several of the farmhands who happened to be present. 'Whoi, didden yew know as our shepherd were a blond?' they choroused, slapping their knees and rocking from side to side in simple fun.

Both the shepherd and his pretty, rosy wife came from Clunford, and he often used to quote to me the couplet,

'Clunberry, Clunford, Clungunford and Clun
Are the sleepiest places under the sun,'

85

but she didn't go along with this rendering, and she would say, 'No, Bill, that's not it, that's not right. It ought to say,

"Clunberry, Clunford, Clungunford and Clun
Are the four *best* places under the sun"

that's more loyal, like.'

Five hundred lowland ewes is a lot for one man to look after, even with the help of an assistant. Bill managed it somehow, but the one who felt the overwork most of all was his dog, Towser. Towser was a nondescript shorthaired kind of sheepdog, mostly black; but during my pupilship he was showing signs of strain, which manifested itself in a series of fits, and the shepherd was on the lookout for a replacement dog. A useful dog with sheep is harder to come by than you might expect, however, unless you have a fairly deep pocket, and Towser had to soldier on meanwhile as best he might.

The sheep were divided into three main flocks. There were the Cluns, or Clun Forests, to give them their proper name. These were middle-sized sheep, with black or dark-brown faces and legs. Lighter than the classic old-fashioned arable farm breeds like the Suffolk, the Clun has proved itself so excellent that it is often taken as the standard by which other 'grassland' breeds are judged. Fecundity, milkiness and good mothering are all qualities for which the breed is known, and the quality of the fleece, too, is noteworthy. Crossing with a down ram, such as a Dorset or a Hampshire, gives progeny with the potential for quick growth and heavy fleshing in the right areas; the milkiness of the mother, her ability to take advantage of a good pasture, gives the offspring the opportunity to express this potential, and many a Clun lamb is ready for the butcher at the tender age of twelve to fourteen weeks.

Another local breed was the Kerry Hill, a smarter sheep, maybe, with its black nose and spotted face and legs. A Kerry ram on a Welsh ewe is the cross that brings the locally popular spreckle-face; crossed again with a down ram, this too brings a useful butcher's lamb that will be able to fatten while still on its mother's milk.

But pride of place in the Rook's Moat sheep was surely held by the Scotch halfbreds. This is a cross known for many years,

86

that became intensely fashionable after the war, with the result that good ewes of the type became prohibitively expensive. But they were 'wuth it to look at yet', as the Yorkshire saying goes; their tall ears, sharply pricked, inherited from their Border Leicester father, and their neat, cobby bodies and fine white legs following their hardy Cheviot mothers. A down ram was chosen for their husband too, and it was pretty to see the little dark-faced lambs skipping among the stylish all white ewes.

I once asked Martin why he had this penchant for Scottish animals, with his Ayrshire cows and Scottish halfbreds, when there were so many good English breeds to choose from. 'Oh! that's straightforward enough!' he replied. 'I don't say they're any better than any English breeds, but they're just as good and I simply love going up to Scotland to buy replacements!'

A fair acreage of the farm was in corn or roots, and various outlying parcels of land were grazed by bunches of bought-in stores. It was a truly mixed farm, in the best sense of the word, and I reckoned I was lucky to be there. Everything was done properly and in order, and there was a bit of everything to be done.

After a week or two, life settled down into a routine and I found myself happier than I had ever been. Awakening at six or earlier, I would leap out of bed, and climb into my overalls before getting down on my knees. This was not done in the cause of devotion, but took the form of a preliminary scan of the weather, so that I could decide if I needed to take my jacket to work or not. My little room was tucked up in the roof space of the guest house, at the back, and the window was at floor level. Not that I found this in any way a disadvantage; for just outside my window was a great tall pear tree, and to look into its topmost branches, seeing the blossom, as it were, face to face, was a constant delight.

Creeping downstairs, my boots in my hand, I would gently lift the catch of the kitchen door and take the thick slice of bread, kept fresh between two plates, that had been left ready for me the night before. Then I would let myself out of the back door, and walk up the narrow street of the village, marvelling, as I munched, at the freshness of the morning, and greeting the other early risers who, like me, were on their way to a day's work.

The others would be there by the time I arrived at the farm; Jean would be assembling the milking machines, and Gosling and Lesley, the boy, would be fetching the cows, who poured into the cowshed in a brown and white dappled stream and separated to go each to her own place, where they stood, waiting to be tied up. Occasionally something went wrong. One day, someone had failed to put into place the bar that stopped them going up the lane, and although the first twenty or so arrived, the others failed to materialise. I was tying cows in one of the little overflow cowsheds, and when I looked out and saw all the tails disappearing from view, I did what seemed obvious. Shutting the door to prevent the ones I had not yet tied getting out, I slipped up the field beside the lane at the double, and, coming out of a gateway in front of the errant cows, turned them, and brought them back to the yard in good order. I thought I had done rather well in fetching them with so little trouble, and half-looked for a word of praise for my promptitude. But any such expectations were quickly dashed when I got back to the yard, for there was the Goblin dancing up and down and positively trembling with rage, angrier than I'd ever seen him. You!' he said. 'You! Elizabeth! Never do that thing again! Never again, do you hear me?' It turned out that my crime had been to shut the small cowshed door, with some cows inside tied up, and some loose. The majority of the cows had their horns on in those days, and apparently the tied-up ones might have suffered frightful damage from the loose ones, who could have taken the opportunity to horn them from behind with impunity. None had, however, and though I hung my head and learned my lesson I did think that the Goblin was making rather a meal of the whole matter.

On ordinary days when the cows came in normally, we tied them up, and the milking started. From cow to cow we moved, up one side and down the other of the modern fifty-tie cowshed, washing, fore-stripping and putting the units on the udders of the cows, who stood calm and complacent, munching the ration of sweet fresh mixture that was put before each one as she was milked. The particular kind of milking machine we used on that farm had a little glass section at the base of each teat-cup, so it was easy to see when the milk stopped flowing as the udder emptied. Then you pulled down slightly on the machine to extract the last bit of milk, before turning off the air-tap and releasing the suction that held the teat-cups on. As each bucket filled, you changed the lid, with the working bits on it, over to a spare, and the full bucket was emptied through a strainer, into a churn.

Before we reached the half-way stage of the milking, Martin would join us, and would say to Jean and me, 'Right, you two; you can go down and make a start on the cartoning.' And off we would go. The farm supported quite a substantial retail milk round, and the milk was delivered to the customers in one-pint cartons with metal clips across their tops. The processing of the milk to the stage where it was ready for delivery took place in the second room of the dairy, adjacent to that where the units were washed and sterilised, and both rooms were permeated with a beautiful smell. It had many components; the hypochlorite which was used for washing the units—the steamy smell of the sterilising cabinet; and, above all, the faint, fresh scent of the milk itself, cool, frothy and abundant. This bouquet for me will always symbolise a modern dairy farm, just as the sweet mixture of hay and cows' breath epitomises and old-fashioned one.

As each churn was filled in the cowshed, one of the milkers rolled it down to the dairy, where Jean and I received it. The first thing to do was to cool it, and this was done by running it over a cooler, a device like an old-fashioned rubbing-board with cold water constantly coursing through its tubes. As it was a well-organised sort of farm, the cooler water ran out through a hose that went out of the window and debouched into a tank in the yard outside. When Bert, the milkman, had finished his second round of the day, he brought the electric milk float round there, and used this ample store of water to wash it to a shining pitch of perfection. At least he usually did. He was thwarted one day because I, disconnecting the hose from the cooler at the end of one milking, let it slide out of the window and lie on the ground. The result was that when Bert rolled up with his bucket and shammy, he was confronted by an empty tank. It was my first introduction to the principle of siphonage; I thought it was terribly sneaky.

Raising the milk to the vat above the cooler was quite a feat of strength, and at first I thought I could never do it. But soon I began to feel more confidence in my own strength, and in a week or two I was slinging a five-gallon churnful more than head-high just as casually as Jean did.

The cartoning machine had a vat, too, but a smaller one than the cooler. Jean was the ace cartoner, and worked up a speed, by dint of much time-and-motion study, that I could never rival. I usually worked the little machine that clamped the clips on, and stood to get Bert's curses if they weren't tight enough, so that they came off in his hand while he was delivering.

Any surplus milk was sent in churns to the creamery, and as it was Grade A Tuberculin Tested (not universal in those days) it had to be sealed in the churns with a lovely little soft lead pellet that you hammered flat on a loop of string. I was looking forward to playing with this toy when we became farmers ourselves; it was a disappointment to discover that the practice had been discontinued.

After milking came breakfast, and after breakfast, machine-washing and cowshed cleaning. When that was over, we awaited our orders for the day—at least, we pupils did. (There were two male pupils, besides me. Jean had a series of jobs to see to round the yard, feeding calves, bulls, and so on.

There was no lack of variety in the work that Martin sent us out to do. He used to drive around his somewhat scattered acres in a jeep, and if we were working in one of the outlying bits of the farm, he would deliver us there and hand us over to whoever was in charge, while he went off to do something else. You never knew what your day's work might be. It might be: 'Elizabeth! You're going up to Blacklees today, you can be horsehoeing those mangolds with the bailiff up there,' when you would spend the day hanging on to the bridle of a most stupid bay mare trying to ensure that she walked down the row and didn't put her great plate-like feet on the shiny green mangold plants, as the scuffler tore gently through the earth, and buried the chickweed and the fathen beneath a shower of fine, dark mould.

Or 'Hoeing—swedes—Will'll show you how to do it', which meant labouring up and down the field chopping out the weeds with a bent-necked hoe, while all the pains of hell got hold upon your bowed back, and your fellow-workers took advantage of your slowness to have a nice rest at the end of each row.

'Go and help the shepherd today,' was a popular order. I liked the shepherd with his steady, kindly ways, and his quiet country sense of humour. I remember one day we were treating some weaned lambs for 'Orfe', a virus complaint related to the cold-sore one that troubles some human beings. It is more serious in sheep, for a bad outbreak brings up scabby, sore swellings on their lips and nostrils until they find it difficult to eat or even to breathe—when, naturally enough, they lose condition.

These lambs had a patchy sort of outbreak, in that some of them had escaped, some were slightly affected, and a few were pretty bad. I had to catch those that needed treatment, and drag them to the shepherd, and he painted the sores with some medicament and put them into another pen. It was easy at first to pick out the bad ones, but there were about 150 in the bunch, and after a couple of hours I thought we'd done all that was necessary.

'That's the lot,' I said, hauling up yet another struggling adolescent. The shepherd looked dubiously at the remainder. 'What about that one?' he said, indicating another sufferer that had escaped my eye. I caught it, with some difficulty, and dragged it up to him. 'That's the last, I'm sure now,' I said. But the shepherd was not convinced. 'You get back in there, girl, and have a real proper look round,' he said. 'You said he wasn't there just a minute ago!'

But though I enjoyed working with the shepherd, the favourite command was 'Elizabeth, you can come with me today.' It was always so interesting going round the farm with Martin. You learned something all the time. 'We'll go down to the fields by the kennels and have a look at that re-seed first,' he might say; and when we got there, he made nothing of my anxieties about a nasty-looking weed infestation that seemed to be swamping the new grass. 'Lamb's tongue, that's all it is—nothing to worry about! I might put the mower over it, but I don't think

91

I'll need to at that. In a week or so we'll turn those Hereford bullocks in, and they'll soon graze it off, you'll see.' We inspected the Hereford bullocks next, as they grazed in an adjoining field. They had only recently been bought, and Martin was keeping a very careful eye on them, for they had come from a poor farm, and there was risk of bloat on the richer pastures of Rooks Moat. He showed me how to look at them from behind to see whether the rumen was swollen with gas enough to show higher than the backbone on the left-hand side; luckily for my education, there were two that were slightly bloated, so we drove them into the shed in the field, and later on Martin came down again and dosed them.

Or we might drive up into the hills to the hundred acres of rented grazing. This was part of a scheme launched by the government for the reclamation of marginal land; it stood out strangely from the surrounding moorland, fenced with wire into neat squares. A healthy growth of grass showed what the land was capable of, when limed and re-seeded.

During my pupilship, a new venture was started on this piece of land. With Martin's penchant for Scottish breeds, it was hardly surprising that when he came to found a suckler herd he should choose the Aberdeen Angus. A whole herd was purchased in Scotland, and trucked down to Rook's Moat—about forty head in all. They arrived in rather poor condition, having spent the last few months on a highland deer forest, and their care in the early days posed rather a problem. All the Drivers' land was really rather too good for them; they could certainly not have been put straight on the reclaimed land without risk of bloat and other stomach troubles. In the end they were started on a field down by the kennels where the big Hereford bullocks had already eaten the best of the grass. There they were inspected a couple of times a day, and as their condition improved, they were moved in small bunches, up to their permanent home.

Their husband, an Angus bull called Meadows Knight, had already been at the Blacklees farm for a couple of years. His job there had been to run with the Ayrshire heifers that were being reared as herd replacements, to get them in calf. He never said 'boo' to a goose, or roared, or pawed the ground, or anything the least bit terrible, and I always thought he was a sweet old thing. Watkins didn't think so, however, later on that winter, when the bull was boxed down at the farm and it suddenly turned on him. It wasn't Watty's fault; he had gone in with the animal's food as usual, and as he tipped it into the manger, suddenly there was this great chunk of ambulant beef trying to crush him against the end wall. I don't know how Watty got out—he was not, you would have said, a man built for sprint work—but before he could clap the door to, the bull was out in the yard with him, kneeling on him and trying to grind him into the earth with its head. Very luckily, the site it chose for this operation was a big heap of strawy manure, and the harder it pushed, the deeper Watkins sank in. Even so, it broke his arm for him before the other workers heard the commotion and came to drive it off him with pitchforks. And this was a quiet, placid bull without the benefit of horns (the Angus being a naturally polled breed). It is as good an illustration as I know of the fact that there is no such thing as a trustworthy bull.

It was fun driving around in the jeep in the sun and the wind, inspecting things. One day when we were going along quite fast, I saw a little movement at the hole in the floor where the accelerator pedal went through. It was a mouse. It climbed half-way out, looked around under the seats and among the pedals, and then withdrew, with quiet deliberation. When we stopped, I looked underneath to try to see where it could possibly have lodged, but there hardly seemed room for an earwig down there, let alone a fat, complacent mouse.

I gave Martin a bad fright in the jeep one day, and myself too. He had turned it off the road into the entrance gateway of Blacklees and got out to open the gate. I slipped across into the driving seat, and said, 'Can I have a go? It isn't on the king's highway here, after all.' Being a kindly man he said yes, and climbed into the passenger seat. But what I hadn't realised was that the wheels were still screwed round in a right-angle turn—and when I revved up the engine and let in the clutch with a bang, instead of jerking forward along the track, the jeep bounded away to the right and started ascending the steep roadside bank at about forty miles an hour. I was rigid with panic, and in the terror of the moment kept my foot firmly jammed down on the accelerator. What a noise and confusion there was! I was screaming, Martin was shouting, and the Land-Rover engine was revving at the top of its powerful voice. Martin thrust a leg out of the doorway and propped the jeep from rolling over, and eventually we completed our arc and arrived back on the road again, rather the worse for wear. I don't know how I looked—red, I should think! but Martin was white and bedewed with sweat, and clouds of black smoke were pouring out of the jeep's exhaust. It took away all my enthusiasm for learning to drive in a moment.

As well as the useful stock on the farm, there were several riding horses and ponies. Martin enjoyed a bit of horse-coping, and the best treat of all was when you were told the night before, 'Be sure and have clean shirt and breeches ready tomorrow. We're going to such-and-such a horse fair.'

We would set off after an early breakfast in our riding clothes, and a merry carful we would be as we drove the twenty-odd miles through the charming Shropshire countryside. Sometimes we had a catalogue to peruse and mark—sometimes we had to rely solely on our judgement. The other pupils rode occasionally, and enjoyed it as a day out, but it was not to them the matter of holy seriousness that it was to me. Horses were my religion in those days, and to strut purposefully among them, pursing knowledgeable lips as I peered at teeth or ran my hand down legs was the apotheosis of bliss. Not that I really knew all that much about them—but that did not matter. Martin of course was the arbiter of what was to be bought, so I could do my pennyworth of showing off without any consequences at all.

We did get some nice animals too, sometimes. Quite early on in my stay there we brought back a little bay gelding of the Welsh Mountain type, christened Rufus, and a 13.2 grey who was called Timmy. Then Martin bought himself a fine big chestnut cob, Robert—and what with Blossom, the shepherd's pony, and Walnut, a funny little long-backed brown mare, we had quite a herd. Sometimes we would all go out together for a pleasant hack round the moorland tracks. Martin rode Robert, and the shepherd rode his own pony. I would have Rufus, and

94

Bert, the milkman, would mount Timmy. Timmy had been trained for country-style trotting races (not the sophisticated kind they have now) and his manners were shocking. As soon as he was mounted he wanted to be off, and would jog and fuss and fidget and sweat, throwing his head up and down and working himself into a lather, which made him a most uncomfortable ride. I worked on him for weeks trying to get him to relax, but even though eventually you could start at a walk, he never learned to accept the aids for the trot without leaping forward as if he was being ridden by Paul Revere.

Sometimes we would build little jumps of poles and brush in the fields, and school the ponies over them in the evenings. Walnut was an excellent jumper for her size; she flipped over anything with a notable economy of effort, making all the other ponies look incompetent by comparison. One evening, sailing casually over an obstacle, she burst her girth with a pop, and saddle and rider flew off in an elegant arc. It was not me that time, though; the unfortunate victim was a boy called Alan, who lived in the village, and often came out with us on his pretty bay filly, Betty. He was not hurt, and, borrowing a girth, he took her over it again.

Not all the horses were bought at fairs. A gypsy of indeterminate age, called Colman, used to come by the farm several times a year in the course of his wanderings; he was quite an old friend, and was always allowed to park his caravan and graze his horses in a retired green lane up in the area of the Blacklees farm. He did not look at all like my pre-conceived idea of a gypsy, being neither swarthy nor dark-haired. Nor was he hawk-faced; nor did he wear a gold ear-ring. At first glance, he looked something like a groom in a middling kind of situation—small and thin, with a wrinkled skin and a quiet style of address. He wore leggings and breeches, and a flat cap. When we heard that he was in the area, we went up to see him, for he usually had one or two horses with him that were for sale.

I do not remember much about Colman's caravan, or the family that he presumably had travelling with him. The thing above all that sticks in my mind is the fact that the only horses that were not on offer were the skewbalds. One, in particular— a dour, heavy-headed animal with a flapping underlip—was

95

the apple of his eye. It was the one that drew the caravan, and he assured us many times that he would never part with it. It looked so unremarkable that I for one felt no urge to put his sincerity to the test by making him an offer. This preference of gypsies for 'coloured' horses is very noticeable; they can have them, for me—but then, as Welsh people always say at a difference of opinion, 'It's lucky we aren't all the same, isn't it?'

The horse that Martin bought from Colman during my pupil-ship was an oldish brown gelding of about fifteen hands who proved to be an amiable enough creature, though nothing much of a jumper. He was christened Jorrocks. One day Martin was approached by a young man who had recently come to live in the village, and asked if he had any horses to hire, so Jorrocks was offered, and a time was fixed. I was instructed to get the horse up, clean, and saddled for the occasion, which I did, and in due course our hero arrived, nattily arrayed in breeches, boots and bowler, with a pair of yellow string gloves, and a very professional-looking hunting whip. I held the horse while he mounted, and adjusted his stirrups to the proper length, but I must say I had my doubts about his prowess as I watched him ride out of the yard. It seemed to me that he was riding on altogether too loose a rein. However, mine not to reason why; I was well aware I wasn't too hot a performer in the saddle my-self, and besides, my advice hadn't been asked.

But my suspicions were all too well founded, and within a quarter of an hour he clattered back into the yard, trotting very fast and nearly falling off as Jorrocks swung dangerously round the gatepost, his big hooves slipping around on the stones. Seeing the haystack, Jorrocks trotted briskly up to it, stopped abruptly and began to eat. Off tumbled his rider, glad enough, from the look on his face, to be on terra firma again, and, hand-ing over the reins, announced that he had decided not to ride that day after all. He was not feeling very well. 'Well, we can't charge you for such a short ride,' I said. 'Perhaps some other time?' 'Yes, indeed!' he said heartily, before skipping past the gatepost and passing out of my life. Or almost; now I come to remember, I did have one more conversation with him. He was doing some kind of social work in the village, and, seeing him coming out of a house as I was on my way back to the guest house, I walked along with him for a bit. 'I've just been visiting Mr. X,' he volunteered, by way of conversation. 'He's a most interesting man, I find. Do you know, last night I was there and he made a special point of taking me out into the backyard so that he could show me his nine-inch collapsible telescope?' A memorable remark.

It was Bert, the milkman, who told us the full tale of his Mazeppa-like ride. 'I was delivering at that cottage by the cross-roads, just outside the village, and I saw him coming along. I saw it was old Jorrocks, so I just waited, to see how he'd get on. He was walking, all anyhow, you know—"here's-me-arse and there's-me-arse", we used to call it—with the horse's head nearly between his knees, and him sitting back, with his feet stuck out. And then when he came to that bit of green at the crossroads, Jorrocks puts his head down, and starts to graze. So my lord hauls him up a couple of times, but down he goes again. So then he hit him with that crop, on the shoulder. And that did it! Old Jorrocks lays his ears back and flicks up his back legs, then he whips round with him and sets off for home, with that silly Herbert hanging round his neck. I'm surprised he made it back to the farm.'

The three smallest ponies were kept in a paddock adjoining the buildings, and as they were all easy to catch, we often used them for local transport around the farm, or down the village. 'Elizabeth, just slip down to the Willow Field and bring up those nine in-calf heifers—but gently, mind! Don't hurry them, they're all heavy in calf,' Martin might say. So, pulling a halter over Rufus's ears, I clattered across the road, and cantered down the gentle slope, two or three fields in, to where they were grazing. We never bothered with saddles or bridles for a job like this; both Rufus and Walnut would neckrein, and Rufus, indeed, was so responsive that he could be steered by the very swing of your body. I often rode him in this way to fetch stock, but the incident of the in-calf heifers stays in my mind because they made such a fool of me. Thinking not to excite them, I got off Rufus, and began to shepherd them gently towards the gateway, but they had other ideas. They were young; the air, sparkling with frost and sun, was exhilarating;

97

and being fetched from their field by a girl with a pony was a wonderfully exciting experience. So with fine disregard for my orders, they poured, frisking, out of the gate, and galloped, mooing and bucking like mad things, all the way up to where Martin was leaning over the gate awaiting them. To do him justice, he didn't blame me. 'I suppose if they do it of their own accord it won't do them any harm,' he said. 'I just hope so, anyway!' It was all right, as it turned out. They all calved down at their due dates, and not one slipped a calf, which is what he was afraid of.

I used to ride Rufus down to lunch sometimes, when I was a bit late. I would tie him in the shed, and he would wait, patiently enough, until my hour was up. I was something of a trial to the proprietors of the guest house in the matter of lateness for meals. I didn't own a watch, and would, in any case, have been far too diffident to suggest that it was my lunch hour. But usually my lateness was only a matter of ten or fifteen minutes; only once did I get the real big frown treatment for being over an hour late, and that was hardly my fault.

As well as the two adjoining farms and the hundred acres of reclaimed land, the Drivers owned various parcels of land about the place, and I was often sent out on a pony to count and check the welfare of bunches of animals grazing these outlying fields. One such was a mixed bunch of steers and dairy replacements, living in some fields down near the blacksmith's forge, about two miles outside the village. I was riding Timmy that day, properly, with a saddle and bridle, and I was quite pleased with him. There was a long, straight, flat stretch of road on the way, and for once in a way, I had managed to get him steadied down to a nice quiet workmanlike jog as we went along it.

I jumped off him when we reached the gate, and tied him up. There were two adjoining fields, with the gate open between them, and a stream, and a strip of woodland. It was a nice piece of ground for the cattle, and normally they were spread out all over it, so that I had to hunt round for them, to check that they were all right, and that they were all there. But today was different. I saw the moment I climbed over the gate that there was something unusual. They were all gathered in a tight mob in the middle of the field, and they were looking very intently at something—upwards, as far as the conformation of their necks would allow them.

And when I followed the direction of their gaze, I, too, saw what was intriguing them. For one of the trees was on fire. It was nothing excessively dramatic—no roaring tongues of flame or fountains of sparks, but a good thick column of smoke was rising from a tangled mass of twigs that might have been a crow's nest, about thirty feet above ground, and an occasional little explosion of crackling showed that the fire was only waiting for a bit of a breeze before really getting hold and showing us what it could do. For a moment I pondered my course of action. Ought I to try to climb up and put it out myself? But common sense soon put a damper on that idea. I am the sort of person who goes pale and faint on a six-foot step-ladder, and this tree was a tall, slender sapling, with a long bare trunk and all its twiggery at the top. There was no farm any-where within sight where I could ask for help; the only thing to do was to go back to Foxwood as fast as I could and get Martin, hoping that meanwhile it would not have blazed up into a proper forest fire.

I think Timmy was surprised by our homeward journey. It was the same person on his back who was always trying to relax him and slow him down, and now she was encouraging him to step out along the road as if he was back in his old trotting-racing days. Where the turf road verge was wide enough, he was even required to gallop! It was all most puzzling. We made good time back to Rook's Moat, and clattered briskly through the town, my legs aching with posting to the trot. I delivered my dramatic news just as Martin was sitting down to his lunch, and though he looked at me as if I was mad when I said there was a tree on fire out there, he rose without demur from the table, and said he supposed he'd better come and see what I was talking about.

Timmy was returned to the paddock, and Martin and I drove out to the fire in the jeep. It was still burning away quite briskly, even sending out occasional shoots of flame by now. I wondered how Martin would deal with it, but he was in no difficulty. He had brought a long piece of rope with him, and he fastened one end round the tree, and the other to the back of the jeep. Then, engaging the four-wheel drive, he drove slowly away and, to my surprise, the jeep plucked the tree out of the ground like a rotten tooth and brought it crashing down. Of course it was simple enough to put the fire out once we could get at it at ground level, and the only thing that remained to do was to speculate as to how it could possibly have caught fire in the first place.

There are two theories that strike me as possible. One is that the crow or magpie in whose nest the blaze started had carried home a piece of broken bottle or some other curved glass, and that the sun's rays, being concentrated through it, had started the blaze. The other is that the bird had been 'anting'. This is a strange activity that many birds practice, when they catch live ants and tuck them into their armpits, indulging in a curious range of ecstatic movements meanwhile, which are quite unmistakable once you have seen a bird performing the ritual. The ants, outraged, presumably emit drops of formic acid which stimulate the bird in some way; the only practical reason for it seems to be that the formic acid is deleterious to the feather-mites, which are parasitic on the bird. I saw a green woodpecker anting once, and if I hadn't previously seen photographs of birds so turned on, I should have thought it was suffering from brain damage. But the relevance of anting to our tree fire is that birds don't limit themselves to ants when they are looking for something stimulating to put in their armpits. Their point of view is that it doesn't matter what it is as long as it hurts, and birds have been observed on several occasions anting with lighted cigarette stubs. Admittedly, they don't usually ant at the nest, but it is possible that a stub, picked up after being thrown from a passing car, could have been carried home for a bit of delayed ecstasy.

But ant me! was I late for lunch!

Horses, of course, were only playthings, useful though we found them for these odd jobs about the farm. Our real business there was to learn about cattle and sheep, particularly the former, and most of our time was spent around them.

This was no hardship to me; I had always liked cows, and it was particularly interesting now to have their choice and nurture expounded by somebody who knew a lot about it. It had its lighter side, too. Martin was in the cowshed one afternoon, looking over a couple of new-bought cows that were tied up there, and we three pupils were with him. An impromptu seminar on the points of the dairy cow developed, and Martin waxed eloquent on the special characteristics of his beloved Ayrshires. He showed us the escutcheon at the back of the bag; he demonstrated what was meant by the 'dairy wedge'. Then he turned his head to say 'Do you see what I mean?' but the ungrateful cow chose that moment to raise her tail, and with cynical opportunism she defecated neatly and exactly between his shin and his wellington boot. After he'd been saying such flattering things about her too! It is a good thing that he was such a nice-natured man.

Quite often, Martin would take us to cattle markets, sometimes to buy, and at other times just to look and learn. Far be it from me to say that markets are perfect yet, but I will aver that animals went through a much more savage hell in markets when I was young than they do now. Almost everybody had a stick in his hands in those days, and used it thoughtlessly and all the time. Two old chaps sitting gossiping on the railings by the cattle pens would keep their right arms busy all the time, automatically hitting every beast that passed, whether it was doing what was wanted or not. I found it sickening to hear the constant, needless crack of knobby wood on knobby bone. I can only assume that they liked hitting the stock in the same way that a batsman enjoys a cracking cover drive. If they didn't enjoy it, they certainly martyred themselves.

The other thing that was worse then than now was the degree of 'bagging up' that was indulged in. A freshly calved dairy cow must be sold with a full bag—convention demands it—and is never milked later than mid-afternoon on the day before the sale; but some of the poor creatures in those days were 'stocked' until their bags were nearly bursting, and waddled along in the grossest discomfort, with hind legs widely splayed, and milk jetting from their teats at every step. The R.S.P.C.A. makes sure that nobody goes in for excessive bagging up now—there is a notice at every cattle market warning everybody that it is illegal.

101

It was fun to walk with Martin and the other pupils round Shrewsbury market, choosing the cows you would buy if you had the money. I used to wear my 'good suit' for cattle markets, because we occasionally went for tea to a pleasant restaurant afterwards, where boots and breeches would have been inappropriate. I always used to think that if I had to live in a town, instead of the country, Shrewsbury would be my first choice. I never got to know it really well, but every time we went there I discovered new beauties in its narrow streets —a gracious, half-timbered house, perhaps, leaning gently over a quiet alley; or a glimpse between buildings, of the shining river, with rowing eights on it, from the famous school.

The terms of my pupilship were that I gave my labour in exchange for the instruction I received; no money changed hands, neither premium nor wages. I felt myself lucky to be on such a pleasant and well-run farm, and in recompense, it seemed to me that I ought not to have much time off. Not that I wanted it, anyway; I so enjoyed the work that I kept waving away the free time Martin offered me, and put in as many as eighty hours a week sometimes ...

The trouble was not the working hours, but the others. For work at the farm did finish after the evening milking, and after I had eaten my high tea at the guest house, there were several hours to be filled in before I could reasonably go to bed, and I couldn't spend every evening writing letters or washing my hair. One of the other pupils used to go out shooting over the farm fields in the evenings, and I overcame my shyness enough to ask if I could come round with him sometimes. But he said I couldn't. 'If you had a gun of your own, or even a working dog, it would be different. But it spoils the shooting to have somebody just walking along taking no part in it.' I don't know if this is true, or if it was just the old business of excuse, excuse; but it left me very much where I was as far as evening entertainment was concerned.

So I took to going for walks by myself about the fields, in which I revelled to the full in a pleasurable kind of literary melancholy. Sometimes I imagined I felt like Anne Elliott—but no, that personality did not fit; I was not old enough to consider

102

myself disappointed, nor did I want to lay claim to her gentle, submissive obedience. The scholar gypsy, perhaps?

> 'Rapt, twirling in thy hand a withered spray,
> And waiting for the spark from heaven to fall'?

(For years I contended, against my form-mates' derision, that those lines meant that the scholar gypsy was trying to make a fire by means of a fire-drill, as used by Australian aborigines)— but no, I couldn't really pretend that I was like him; he was thinking hard, concentrating on something as he walked along. I was just wandering about. The best fit for me was Keats's Ode to Melancholy—

> 'But when the melancholy fit shall fall
> Sudden from heaven, like a weeping cloud . . .
> Go glut thy sorrow on the morning wave,
> Or on the globed wealth of peonies,
> Or on the rainbow of the salt sea wave—
> Or if thy mistress some rich anger shows,
> Imprison her soft hand, and let her rave,
> And feed deep, deep upon her peerless eyes.'

The bit about the mistress I ignored as irrelevant. I neither had one nor was one—but the rest was authentic. I used to betake myself to a lovely place, a long narrow sheet of water in one of the fields, surrounded by willows (a 'plash' in local terms) and sit there, watching the sun going down, and glorying in the ache of my sensibilities. Mute swans nested at one end of that plash, and it was an additional pleasure to watch them taking off and landing. Swimming, they were the epitome of grace, with their sinuously curved necks, and flying, with great wings beating, they were majestic. But in between the two states, coming or going, they had an interregnum of utter bathos. Taking off it took them almost the whole length of the plash to get airborne, and when they had dragged themselves, with mighty wingbeats, almost clear of the water, their ridiculous back legs would appear, pedalling like mad until lift-off was finally achieved. Landing was even sillier. They would come in at great speed, and plane down, on stiffly arched wings, with both feet stuck out in front of them. A great furrow of water would be kicked up as they hit; they looked exactly as if they were skidding along the surface of the water on their feathery bums. A good performance by the swans always made it difficult for me to sustain my melancholy mood, and I would go home to my little room under the eaves lighthearted again.

Sunday evenings, however, were never lonely, for after evening church I would go back with the Drivers to their house The Grove for supper.

I don't know what became of the original farmhouse of Foxwood Farm. It just didn't seem to exist. The family lived in The Grove, which was a charming house, only about forty yards along the road from the farm. But it was certainly not built as a farmhouse. It was several hundred years old, with a large garden and a cluster of outbuildings, and I should guess was probably originally constructed for some rich merchant or burgher of Rook's Moat.

The dining-room was sombre but handsome, panelled from floor to ceiling in oak, in a plain pattern, which, with hindsight, I would attribute to the second half of the seventeenth century. Here, every Sunday evening, we sat round an immense gate-legged table, and got outside the sort of supper that most of England only dreamed of in those days. It was 1948, with food still rationed, and lots of things not available. But farmers were in a better position than many people, and the table at The Grove groaned with hospitable cheer. Among the Ayrshires, there was one single Jersey, and her milk was always put on one side for 'The House'. Then, on Saturday evening, Martin would put a few gallons of it through the separator, and the resultant abundance meant that there was no shortage of cream or butter. I particularly remember the cream, because there was such a lot of it. It was passed round the table in a big quart jug, and, naturally, it tasted only of cream, and not of cardboard, as bought cream is inclined to do.

After a while, I got to know the vicar and his wife and their three young children, and I used to spend many of my evenings with them. My guest house was right down by the church; it only took a minute to slip across after tea, and once there, I felt as if I had entered a second home. The house was lovely— old, again, with great wide hand-sawn oak planks in the upstairs floors, polished by centuries of beeswaxing until they shone like black water, and so sloping that the beds had to have their ends propped up to give any approach to a level at all. If you dropped your tin of Nivea onto the floor when you were lying in bed creaming your face, the chances were that it would roll right across the room and end up in the opposite corner. There were lots of little steps up and steps down, and odd little corridors and housemaids' cupboards and boxrooms and attics; it gave the impression of a house that had grown gradually, having new bits added on as the need arose.

The need that dictated such a big, rambling house must have included a number of children and a fair staff of servants; the house was far too big for a family of five, and I am sure the work of such a great place pressed very hardly on Helen, the vicar's wife. She was a beautiful woman, and charming too—but vague—I remember her remarking to me one frosty evening in early May, 'I'm sure one of these days I'll find out that I've tucked some straw round the children and read a bed-time story to the tomatoes!'

Helen was a trained horticulturist, having qualified at Swanley, and the vast garden of the vicarage was both a joy and a torment to her. The previous incumbent had been a keen gardener, and had planted lots of lovely things. It was in that garden that I was first introduced to hardy cyclamen, which were naturalised beneath a great row of beeches between the house and the church. I had never heard of such a thing; cyclamen, for me, meant the big, scentless florists' cyclamen, grown in pots for indoors, and I could hardly believe my eyes when Helen first showed me the tiny bunch of deep pink miniature flowers she had picked. I could hardly believe my nose either, for they were as sweetly scented as violets. They were probably cyclamen europaeum.

But the man who had planted all these things had had a private income, and a gardener, and I know Helen minded the fact that she and John, her husband, could not keep up the whole two acres in the state to which it had been accustomed.

Another thing I learned about from John and Helen was omelettes. I can't think why we never had them at home; it wasn't because of the war-time shortage of eggs, for we kept our own hens, and were never really short. But we never did have them, and when they burst into my life in my eighteenth year I was aware of a similar set of emotions to those that Keats claimed he experienced on first looking into Chapman's *Homer*. I have always meant to look into that myself to see if it would do anything for me, but so many things get overlooked in one's daily round of business that I have never got around to it.

So, with the lengthening evenings filling themselves with riding and visits to the vicarage, my Keatsian melancholy diminished and I became exceedingly happy.

One job which usually fell to my lot, and which I thoroughly enjoyed, was taking the various horses and ponies to the forge. To the forges, I might say, for we patronised two. One, near the fields where the tree went on fire, belonged to a crusty old Yorkshire blacksmith, called Scales; the other, up in the moors in the general direction of the reclaimed land, was run by a gigantic man called Rory.

It was a longish job getting a horse shod in those days, for smiths of good repute did not use the horse-shoe 'blanks' that seem to be universal today, but wrought the shoe from straight iron bar, which was much more interesting. Arriving at the forge, you would slip the saddle off your horse's back for his comfort, and lead him into the smithy, carefully, walking backwards in front of him to make sure he didn't bang his hip on the doorpost. Scales would greet you with a grunt, which by experience you got to know meant 'good morning'. Then, slapping down his wooden box of tools on the floor, he would pick up the first foot, and get to work on it. Our animals were all quiet to shoe, and never demurred at anything he did.

A blacksmith wears a leather apron, and grips the horse's foot between his knees to hold it firm. The first job was to remove the old worn-out shoes; this was done by cutting off the bent-over bits of the shoeing nails where they showed round the front of the hoof. A little tap with a hammer, and the chisel bit neatly through the bright metal, leaving a series of small holes where the nail had been gripping. When all the nails had been dealt with, it was the work of a moment to wrench the shoe off with the big pincers and fling it, clatter and clang, onto the great heap in the corner which awaited the scrap metal merchant.

Then the foot was prepared for the new shoe. A horse's hoof, of course, grows continually, and when shoes need replacing— say, after eight weeks—there is a good deal of horn to be cut away. The first rough section is taken off crudely with a big pair of round-ended clippers; and the final shaping is done with a wicked-looking bent-bladed little hoof knife. The foot must be so trimmed that the new shoe, while taking the wear on the front part of the foot, allows the 'frog', the spring pad at the back of the foot, to have adequate contact with the ground. The frog is part of the horse's shock-absorbing system, and keeping it healthy is a lot of what good shoeing is about.

It is a curious fact that dogs simply love the trimmings of horn from horse's feet, and will dart into the forge to get them with the utmost greediness. I suppose digestive juices that can dissolve ox's thigh-bones are not too daunted by a substance which can be boiled down to glue; but it does look an unappetising tit-bit for all that

With all the feet prepared, the smith turns to making the shoes, while the horse sighs, shifts its weight from one back foot to the other, and rubs its nose messily up and down the front of your shirt. Blacksmiths don't usually like you to tie the horse up—they want you to hold it all the time. I suppose this is because horses have a habit of resting their weight on the blacksmith when he has one of their feet in his lap for several minutes, and it is easier to make them stand up properly from the front than from underneath. This fact often led to a certain awkwardness when I had a horse being shod at Scales's because Martin would say, 'You can slip over and look at the cattle while he's being shod', yet any suggestion of being left alone with the horse produced an outburst of terrifying grumpiness in Scales. 'Aw reet then, aw reet then, you be off! Have it yer own way! But if we're no forrarder when yor get back, doan't blame me, that's all! Yer know ah need yer 'ere! Ah can't do 'im by missen!' It was all nonsense, of course; he could, and did, for, caught as I was between the devil and the deep, I would hold the horse during the foot-preparing, then dash off across country to count the stock while he was making his first shoe.

Arriving back like Pheidippides, I would, with luck, be in time to hold the horse again while he put it on. But if I wasn't in time, he always seemed to have managed well enough.

I was sorry to miss seeing the shoe being made, although I saw plenty of others. After measuring up the foot, the smith would cut a length from one of the long narrow bars of iron that leaned against the wall of his workshop. This came in several gauges, thick for cart-horses, thinner for hunters, thinnest of all for ponies, and he cut off the length quite easily, with one blow of a cold chisel.

Then the bar was seized in the long-handled tongs and pushed into the fire to heat. Holding the tongs in one hand and working the bellows with the other, the smith would create a little snoring heart of red in the dull bank of slack that was his fire in between whiles, and before long, the metal bar would be malleable. Incidentally, the popular concept of a smithy fire as a great, roaring blaze, with sparks flying up the chimney is totally inaccurate in my experience. All the fires I have seen in forges have been tiny, and so dull when the bellows are not in use that you would have had a job to say whether or not the fire had gone out. They do not warm the smithy, either. Most smithies have big double doors that stand open during the working day, and any onlooker who tried to keep himself warm by the fire on a cold day would be so in the way that I'm sure he would be asked to move. A particular kind of small coal is favoured fuel for smithy fires, and the blacksmith sprinkles it on with a shovel, as delicately as you might sugar your strawberries.

Withdrawing the cherry-red metal from the fire, he lays it across the anvil, and knocks the first bend into it. *Tang* ting! ting!, *Tang* ting! ting! For every one heavy blow on the shoe, he hits his hammer directly on the anvil, to knock off the scale that develops on it, in a chemical reaction with the heated metal. Deftly manoeuvring the shoe about with the long tongs, and re-heating it every minute or two, he curves it round, forms the groove beneath it, punches the nailholes, and finally hammers up the toe-piece, one in the centre for a front shoe, two, a bit at the sides, for a back one.

Finally the shoe is ready, and driving a spike into one of the nail-holes from underneath, he carries it over to the patient horse. The shoe is still hot, although not red-hot, and there is a great hissing and a cloud of acrid smoke as he presses it against the underside of the foot. The horse is completely unconcerned by this, knowing from experience that there is no pain in it for him. When the shoe is withdrawn after a few seconds, the smith can see from the scorched horn how it is going to bear on the foot. It may need a minute adjustment, or there may be a soupçon more paring to be done; but, finally, he is satisfied, and plunges it into the water tank to quench it before it is nailed into position. The steam of the hot iron meeting the water joins with the smell of the rasped hooves, the burning horn, and the horse-manure neatly brushed aside, to make up the exciting and wholly characteristic smell of a blacksmith's forge. Then the shoe is nailed on, and the ends of the nails clinched over to hold it firm. A quick rasp round, a wipe of the hoof with an oily rag, and you are ready for off. A complete set of shoes made from scratch like this takes well over an hour —nearer two, perhaps. But it is never dull at the forge. There is a constant stream of people with little jobs for the smith to do—a bent hitch-pin to straighten, an obstinate bolt to unscrew, a broken draw-bar to weld, a hay-knife to sharpen; other horses may be brought, who must wait their turn outside, while their attendant lounges against the doorpost and exchanges local gossip. And if all else fails, there are notices pinned to the door advertising stallions at stud, every one sounding, from the glowing descriptions, a veritable prince of the equine world.

I suppose Scales is dead now; he was an old man in 1948, and an accident he had recently suffered had not improved his health. He had been doing some repair work on the tail-gate of a lorry and was still on it when the driver, thinking he had got off, drove away. 'Ah wor a bit daft, ah can see that now. 'E worn't going very fast, so ah thowt ah'd just jump off, and nowt said. And t'next thing ah knew, ah were wekkin' oop in t'hospital five days later, wi' a grand headache.' The lorry had been travelling at about 35 m.p.h., and of course the old man had been pitched violently forward as his feet hit the ground, and had struck his head on the road, concussing himself badly. He was lucky not to be killed, I suppose.

Rory, the other blacksmith, was younger, and lived in a

much wilder area. It was known as 'The Ship', after the long-since-vanished hostelry. It is hard to imagine what sort of business this pub can have attracted in such a desolate situation up on the moors—it can surely never have provided anyone with their whole living. It was probably worked in conjunction with a small farm, and perhaps it dated from the days of the drove-roads. Thousands of store cattle and sheep used to be driven down every year from the uplands of Wales to be finished on the lusher pastures of England. The drovers were not ill-paid by the standards of the time, and they had to get food, drink and shelter as best they could on the long trek there and back again; so they may have been the customers that justified this lonely pub's existence.

Whatever its origins, by the time I came onto the scene, all traces of The Ship had vanished, except its name, and this was applied indiscriminately to a whole area. One felt a certain caution about the dwellers in The Ship area—at least, I did. They seemed rude in the sense of uncivilised; they spoke a thicker dialect than the people of the lower farmlands, and sometimes I could not understand them. They would shout at you, incomprehensibly, as you rode past, and my manner towards them was always extra-propitiatory.

Rory, too, was a little bit frightening, though being more used to his voice I could usually understand what he was saying. He was a big man, and fat; rumour had it that he was over-fond of the bottle, and often went out in the evening for an alcoholic jolly which was only accounted a thorough success if he finished up unconscious. This could have been inconvenient in many ways if it had not been for one possession that he prized above rubies—a reliable self-drive homing pony. All the landlords of the hostelries he favoured knew how to harness this creature to its little gig, and when saturation point had been reached, and Rory had collapsed, breathing stertorously, onto the floor, it would come into its own. It would be fetched out from where Rory had stabled it on its arrival, harnessed up and pointed in the right direction. Then it would stand patiently, while the gig-lamps were lighted, and the eighteen-stone hulk of its master was heaved in by the landlord and his more sober customers. The reins were knotted up on its neck, and then, at the cry 'All right, Brownie!', with a slap on the rump, off it would go, its little titupping hoof-beats soon lost in the big night, until it brought him safe to his own door. His wife and her sister would be waiting—luckily they were both big, strong, dour, resigned sort of women.

I would sometimes look at this sagacious animal as it grazed behind the forge, and marvel. It was dark brown, very small, and shaggy. It was curious to think of it conducting big, red-faced, shouting Rory home, unconscious, time after time, all by itself. But of course the story may not have been true.

The forge at The Ship was shabbier and more untidy than Scales's, and an extra dimension was added to its bouquet by the big drum of tractor vaporising oil that stood by the door, for sale to the local farmers, who were just beginning to replace their horses with second-hand tractors. Everybody knows how poignantly a smell can recall to us some place or experience long forgotten; and to me, that cool, sweet smell of old-fashioned T.V.O. brings instantly back those farms of long ago, when a farm really was a farm. Perhaps the reek of diesel will stir romantic memories in the children who 'help' in our farmyard now, when they are middle-aged, and when perhaps the advances of science mean that all food is synthesised in giant solar-powered factories!

Scent manufacturers compose their wares like symphonies—a little of this, a touch of that, lovingly concocting and zealously testing. But the finest scent-poem I ever came across was entirely fortuitous, and perhaps that was why it was so lovely.

It was in the granary of a little farm just outside Dolgelley, where we were sometimes allowed to go from school, when exams were finished, to help with the hay. The farmer was an unusual man—a self-taught wild-flower expert, a beekeeper, and a very fine carpenter. He had turned the long granary over the barn into a workshop-cum-storeroom, and the equipment for all his various hobbies was there, each adding its bit to the blend of spicy scents that made up the characteristic bouquet of the room. You could disentangle the component parts with your nose as you lingered there.

First, there were apples. The granary was frost-proof and made a fine store for them, and they sat on the papered shelves in cheerful rows, each kind together, in families, smelling fruity and fresh. Then there was the sawdust. Something was always being made or mended at the big carpenter's bench under the window, and the aromatic resinous scent of the sawn pine or fir pleased the nose as much as the clean, pinkish wood pleased the eye.

Bee-things were there too, with their faint musky, magical odour. Empty honey-combed frames from the extractor, big lumps of melted-down beeswax, spare 'supers', and the dark, clear honey itself, in jars—all redolent of the close, miraculous, million-year-old world of the hive. And finally there was corn, a big open bin of cool, smooth oats, which gave out their remote fragrance as they awaited the moment when they would be shovelled through a hole in the floor into the hopper of the crusher down below.

Foxwood Farm, too, had its lovely farmy smells, and as the year progressed each season brought its own contribution. Hay-making was early in that area, and it was only the end of May when the mower went into the first field. It was very different from any haymaking I had ever helped in before—it seemed so mechanised. Tractors moved to and fro in the fields with tedders and swathe-turners, crossing and re-crossing each other's tracks like country dancers, and in no time, it seemed, the hay was ready to carry.

But this was a different world from the rural simplicities of The Bryn, only five years before. Here there was no potching about with horses and gambos—everything moved more swiftly. A great wooden hay-sweep on the front of the tractor bundled up the windrows of cured hay and brought them to a convenient point in the field, just inside the gate. Here the baler was stationed. The pick-up baler, which travels around the field, had not yet become standard; instead the baler was parked in a convenient place, and the hay was brought up and forked into it, while the bales that emerged from the other end were built into a great long haystack just beside it. When the stack was finished it was covered with a ricksheet, well weighted down with ropes and stones, and the hay was carted down to the stock on the yard during the winter in trailer-loads, as it was required.

Jean and I took some small part in the haymaking, pitching hay into the baler, or taking the bales from the other end and putting them onto the elevator, but we were not really necessary there—there were so many men. Indeed, I often think that the most important difference between the farms of then and now is the plethora of labour that was available then. There must have been twenty men employed at Foxwood—some of them, who habitually worked in the fields or, like the pigman, in outlying groups of buildings, I hardly got to know. They all seemed to me very models of hard work and competence, but old Mr. Driver saw things very differently. Stout, elderly and red-faced, he would stump, puffing, through the fields with a light hoe in his hand, with which to deal with any thistle rash enough to reveal itself, 'keeping an eye on things', as he said. If he found any of the men not actively busy about something— or looking busy, anyway—he would sack them on the spot. 'You can go at the end of the week! Take your money and go! We don't want layabouts here!' he would shout, brandishing the hoe like a rod of authority. But nobody took him very seriously. At the end of the week Martin discreetly re-engaged the dismissed ones, and life pursued its even tenor once again— until the next time.

Old Mrs. Driver, too, believed in getting a pennyworth for a penny, and Bert, the milkman, was her most usual victim. It was not that she caught him slacking—nobody could do that, he was a very bundle of energy, and always went about his duties at a jog-trot—but by about eleven in the morning he would have finished his regular work, and when he took the 'house milk' up to The Grove, she would often be lying in wait for him with a string of little tasks for him that affronted his manliness not a little. I met him one day at about four o'clock stamping back towards the farmyard with a face as black as thunder. 'You look as if you'd lost a shilling and found sixpence,' I told him. 'What's it been today?'

'D'you know what I've been doing since eleven o'clock this morning?' he spat back at me. 'Folding bloody sacks, picking bloody damsons, and cleaning bloody hen-houses! What sort of day's work is that for a man?'

There was work enough for him in July and August, though,

and of a sort that appealed more to his nature. The great, sweeping acres of corn were cut, and we all worked early and late getting them first stooked, and, later, carried. The corn was much taller than any I had seen in Wales; the sheaves were as tall as I was, and when you picked up one under each arm to carry to a stook, the bristly barley-awns brushed against your cheeks bringing on quite a painful rash. 'What's a matter wi' yew, Liz?' the men would call. "Ave yew got stubble trouble, 's that what it is?' Nobody but me seemed to suffer from this problem; perhaps it was because everybody else was taller. We enjoyed working in the cornfields, stooking in a different way from that which I had learned in Wales. There, we stooked in fours, very simply; here there were six sheaves forming a kind of arcade, and two placed flat along the top. It seemed to work just as well, and of course it was quicker when it came to pitching.

With Autumn came the mists, the early evenings, and the great golden rising moons, so much more noticeable at that time of the year. The pear tree outside my window was a fountain of living gold, with the starlings busy about it. They also plundered the apple trees up by the clothes line at the top of the guest-house garden, as I discovered to my chagrin. I had washed some cotton dresses and left them hanging up there overnight, and when I went to get them in I found that they were liberally spattered all over with bird-droppings. This was annoying, but when I re-washed them, I found that it was even worse than it appeared. For where every mess had been, there was now a faded patch, so that my dresses looked as if I was carrying around my own little aura of dappled sunlight. 'Don't string a clothes-line between two apple-trees', says the proverb—a new one which I made up under the stimulus of the event.

The cows grew furry winter coats, and began to be brought in at nights. Winter stores of hay and mangolds were broached; we used to give them two or three big mangolds whole, in their mangers, after milking, and they would scrunch them up like hungry boys eating apples. I can remember those cows so well —Grace, Bunty, Twinkle, Jet, Mist—their names and their faces come easily into my mind's eye. I can remember the cows, indeed, much better than the neighbours; farms were so large

114

in that area that as a lowly farm pupil you never even knew who the neighbours were on some boundaries. Only one other farmer has remained in my mind, and I don't think he was exactly a neighbour. He was a man with a stutter, called Godfrey, and Martin told us one day that he had just met him trying to fish in the river down at the bottom of the village. 'It was all overgrown with big tall thistles, and he was wearing shorts and he was making a damn' bad shot of his casting. He was jumping around from one foot to the other, and cursing and blinding—I should think he must have frightened every fish between here and Shrewsbury. "What's the matter, Godfrey?" I called to him. "Thistles interfering with your fishing tackle?" "N-n-n-no!" he shouts back. "They're damned well interfering with my c-c-c-c-courting tackle!"

PART IV

PENLLWYNPLAN

I

It seems a curious admission to make, but I can't remember now exactly why I changed my mind about reading Agriculture at the university—even about which university I wanted to go to at the end of my year of pupilship. The idea of Oxford had always attracted me, but I never thought I stood a chance of getting a place. What it was in particular that changed my mind enough to make me try is lost in the mists of time. But eventually that is where I found myself, and reading English, not Agriculture. The agricultural stream, indeed, went underground for many years in me, and I have written of its emergence in my first book, *Buttercups and Daisy*. In that book I have described how Desmond, my husband, and I bought Penllwynplan, a sixty-acre holding in Carmarthenshire, and learned, through various ups and downs, to make our living from it. It was different in many ways from the farms of my childhood, Penhallow, Bryn and Foxwood—but it was a real, proper undeniable farm, with cows, manure, hay, hens, cats, and dogs. Every self-respecting farmyard has to be watched over by a dog, and with memories of Fan, Fly, Bright, Towser and all, we have always had one or two about the place since we became farmers.

We brought our first with us from Hertfordshire. She was a tricolour Basenji, called Folly—as pretty as a picture, but destined for a bad end. Basenjis of course are those unusual dogs from the Belgian Congo that never bark. They are not voiceless —they can whine, yelp when trodden on, and 'yodel' in greeting, but the sharp, repetitive 'woof! woof! woof!' is a noise they seem constitutionally incapable of producing.

Basenjis are close-coated animals of about the same size as a fox terrier, with pricked ears, wrinkled brows, and tightly curled-up tails, like a pug's. Most of them are bright red, but Folly was of the recessive colouring, and was mostly black, with long white legs, white chest, and pretty tan markings on her muzzle and eyebrows. The breed standard for Basenjis describes them as 'gazelle-like', and this she certainly was, bounding along with the freest grace and often leaping up to look over the top of long grass or bracken in the style characteristic of the breed. Their African name, indeed—Mbwa Mkwbwa— means literally, 'The jumping up and down dog'.

So Folly came with us to the country, and found the utmost scope for the perfecting of her technique in the tall mowing grass of our new farm. She enjoyed her freedom, but she did not stray, and probably all would have been well if we had not got another dog.

For Folly was not really suitable for farm work. Not being bred for it, she had no idea of herding, and of course being barkless she was not even effective as a watchdog. By the time we had collected a herd of twenty-odd cows, we began to feel the need of a cattle-dog, and we began to look around for one, for cows can be very tiresome on a hot day when for some reason or other they don't want to come from the field for milking, and when you have not got a dog. Usually they come to a call, obediently enough, but occasionally the devil gets into them, and then you could swear that they are co-operating with one another to torment you. You open the gate and emit the traditional cry of 'Trwy! trwy!' About a third of them get to their feet and amble towards you; the rest stay sitting down, chewing the cud with their backs to you. Not wanting the good girls to go on the road unattended, you shut the gate again, and go round to give the sluggards a poke of your stick to rouse them. But, by the time you have got the last one to her feet and travelling in the right direction, the first lot have got tired of waiting by the gate, and have begun to wander away down the field again. And as you dash across to head them off, a little group of the last ones peels off and trots back the way they have come, udders swinging purposefully. I have often felt that a heart-attack must be imminent as I have raced, crimson, up and down a big field, trying to do the dog's work when he has been off on a courting foray. But if he should hear my screamed imprecations, intermingled with his name, and return to his duties, what a change! The instant his familiar form is seen slinking along the hedgerow, the cows know the game is up, and revert to their normal pattern of obedience. Which makes it all the more annoying the next time he is A.W.O.L. and explains the origin of the old phrase 'taking dog's leave'.

We were lucky with our first sheepdog. He came from a farm about a mile up the road—the farm of our neighbour, Norah Lan's father, actually—and he was about six months old when he was given to us. 'I don't want anything for him,' said Mr. Davies, generously, when he offered him to us. 'I just want him to go to a good home. He should turn out a worker— his mother's good, and he's been going round the cattle with her for a month or two. Come and have a look at him one evening, and if you like him, you can take him straight away'.

So that evening, while I put Rachel to bed, Desmond and the three-year-old Matthew went up to inspect the dog. They liked what they saw, and, borrowing a rope to put round his neck, they loaded him into the van. He, poor animal, was terrified. First, there had been the ordeal of being taken into the farm-house kitchen to be looked at. Dogs do not usually cross the threshold, but Mr. Davies wanted Desmond to get a look at him, in a good light, and he was dragged in, rigid with a sense of sacrilege. Then there was the trauma of having a rope knotted around his neck, and of being delivered, bound, into the hands of these barbarians who spoke to him in an uncouth tongue, and bundled him, all unwilling, into the back of a mini van. On the way home, as he crouched on the van floor, his terror reached a climax, and he was overcome. The at-mosphere in the van grew foetid. Matthew looked suspiciously at Desmond and Desmond at Matthew—then, drawing the right conclusion, they each slightly opened their window, and Desmond pressed his foot yet harder on the accelerator.

But the dog had not played his last card yet. When the mini drew up in the yard, and Desmond, holding tight to the end of the rope, encouraged him to jump down, he gave a last, desper-ate wriggle. The rope round his neck slipped up round his ears—

he was free! and, silent as a shadow, he disappeared into the rainy night.

There was a bad start. We took out our torches, and hunted all around, in the hedgerows and around the buildings, but there was no sign of him. Desmond drove back to the farm we had had him from, to see if he had run straight home, but they hadn't seen him. 'But don't worry,' they said. 'Either he'll hang about your place or he'll come back here. We'll let you know if we see anything of him.' So we put out the dinner we had ready for him, in a pie-dish, and went to bed, hoping for the best.

It was dark when we got up in the morning, being October; but sure enough, as the grey light strengthened, there he was, lurking on the churnstand in the rain, looking a picture of misery with his black coat flattened against his sides, and his tail between his legs. I took the untouched dish of dinner down, and encouraged him in my best Welsh with 'cy da! (good dog) and 'derra ma!' (come here); but he declined my advances, and retreated down the road, wagging his tail deprecatingly, but keeping well out of reach. He realised what I had in my hand, though, and when I put it down on the churnstand and stood back, he soon came and gobbled it up.

By lunch-time, his confidence in us was growing, and before nightfall he was so far convinced of our goodwill that we were able to touch him. He spent the night in his own shed, with another good meal and a thick bed of straw, and from then on there was no turning back. He was our dog.

We named him Mot, perhaps the commonest sheepdog name in Wales, but a nice name for all that. My father drew our attention to the story of the black ghost dog in Peel Castle in the Isle of Man, that was known as the Mottie Dhu; Dhu is gaelic for black (Welsh du) and I should not be at all surprised to learn that Mot is a Celtic root-word for dog, though I have no real evidence of it. We often called ours Mottie Dhu as a bit of extra, but, fair play to him, he never frightened anyone to death like his namesake did.

He came fairly close to it, once or twice, though. He turned out to be the sort of dog referred to in dog training circles as a 'hot natural guard', and more than once we had to rescue some timid visitor who was penned up against the garden wall, overawed by the growling and the lavish display of savage-looking white teeth. Another time, he gave a nasty fright to a young woman who had come to buy eggs one evening. The eggs were in the henshed, so I left her in the kitchen with the two young children while I went up to get them. When I came back, she was standing by the kitchen wall tense-faced, and very still indeed, and 'Am I glad to see you!' she said. 'I just went to put my hand on Rachel's head, and your dog came out from under the table—I didn't even realise he was there—growling and snarling; he looked as if for two pins he'd have the throat out of me!'

There were occasions on which he did actually bite people—once the baker's wife, delivering bread, and once a hen customer—but by and large his menace was theory rather than practice. It came in handy, though, when gypsies with white heather or tiresomely importunate carpet-pedlars came to the door. If Mot was in, I would hold him by the collar, and pretend to be having a terrible job restraining him. If not, it sufficed to say 'Watch out for the dog—he's a bit sharp!' One glimpse of him then, sneaking up on the flank, was enough to send them skeltering for the security of their vans, and Mot would usher them out of the yard with a perfect salvo of furious barking.

In his appearance, he was a perfectly ordinary black and white Border Collie. He was large rather than small, and powerfully built, and his head was broad, not snipy. On his muzzle and front legs there was a sprinkling of black spots which made one wonder if there might have been a dash of springer spaniel generations back. His eyes were brown, and, ordinarily, unremarkable. But when he was stroked and petted, he closed them somewhat, and the longer you went on the slittier they became. We called it his Japanese look, and eventually it would become more and more pronounced until he began to look more like a Tojo than a Mot, and the climax would come as he fell over on his back, eyes closed, in a blissful welter of sentimentality.

I am sure that, in the hands of a good trainer, Mot would have made a first-class dog. As it was he didn't do too badly, and this in spite of the disadvantage of three people, all inexpert, training him all at once. Eventually he learned to come when called, to sit and stay, and to walk at heel, though he was never really steady. And in working with the cattle, on his day, he could be brilliant. At other times he would appear to have no idea what you wanted and would drive the cattle away instead of bringing them towards you, or chase one particular cow until the imprecations you were screaming suddenly got through to him, when he would turn towards you with an air of the utmost injured innocence.

Ninety-nine days out of a hundred, though, he performed his simple tasks more than adequately, and it was a joy to send him away up the bank to bring down a stubborn heifer. Having had to toil up there on our own leg-power so many times made us doubly appreciative of his economical power as his great back legs and whippy loins catapulted him up almost without effort. Generally, too, he was good about bringing the cows back temperately; for with many animals giving eight to ten gallons a day, the last thing you want to see is galloping.

Mot and Folly were friends from the start, but it was a friendship that led, indirectly, to her downfall. Using him as her target, she learned to chase, and once the hunting instinct was aroused in so primitive a dog, there was no holding her. Mot, even as a young dog, was much bigger than Folly, but with her long legs and supple back she was an even more superb speed machine than he was, and she soon found she could outrun him. He usually started the game. Bounding up to her, in the field, where she, perhaps, was investigating a tussock of grass, he would give her a nudge with his nose, and then bound away, challenging her to chase him. It was a challenge that was never refused. Gathering herself up like a little ball of black elastic, she would hurl herself down the field after him, and before he had gone fifty yards she would be up with him, and would pull him, at full stretch, to the ground, with her teeth in his shoulder. This bit of it, I must say, he didn't exactly like—and sometimes he yelled piteously as she rolled him over and over. But he never learned to stop turning her on.

The end was foreseeable but, as it turned out, inescapable. One day a neighbour telephoned to say that Folly had been chasing his lambs, and requesting us (reasonably enough) to keep her fastened up. We tried to, although we knew in our hearts that it was no sort of a life for a dog that had grown accustomed to her freedom. But, inevitably, the children accidentally let her out one day, and before we even knew she had gone, she went straight in among a neighbouring flock of sheep, and killed one, as if she had been awaiting her opportunity all the time she had been prevented.

Inevitably, we had to have her destroyed, and though the vet was very unwilling to kill such a lovely young creature, the law was adamant. Luckily it is a very quick death. She was injected into a vein in her front leg, sitting up on the surgery table, and Desmond felt her go limp in his hands before the vet had even finished pressing the plunger.

In addition to losing our dog and paying the value of the fat lamb she had killed, we were fined, as the lamb's owner insisted on taking us to court. However, the fine was only £1, which was not too crippling. But it was sad to lose Folly.

After Folly's death, Mot was our only dog for several years, and very well he filled the position. But he was not faultless. Our farm is situated on the junction between a lane and a road, and a fair amount of traffic passes it, particularly in the summer. Mot, like many another sheepdog on a roadside farm, developed strongly territorial feelings about the farmyard and the piece of road adjacent to it, and his way of expressing these feelings was to fly out barking, in hot pursuit of any vehicle that passed along the road. This is a dangerous habit, but one which is damnably difficult to cure. You can, of course, keep the dog permanently chained up, but Mot always regarded being tied up as a punishment, and showed such acute misery when we tried it that we soon had to relent, and unfasten him. You could easily tell which of the cars that flashed past on the road were driven by local people, because they never swerved, but drove straight on. People who are accustomed to the heart-stopping experience of having a great dog catapult itself at their car realise that this is the safest—indeed, the only—thing to do. The dog is always moving well within its own brake capacity; indeed, a dog which actually chases cars is much safer in traffic than a dog which is unaware of them.

Perhaps it sounds as if I am excusing myself for having been for some years the co-proprietor of a dog which did to some extent constitute a traffic hazard. And I suppose to some extent I must be. For it should be put on record that Mot never caused an accident, and that his dashings-out were no worse than those of several other dogs along the same stretch of road. And while acknowledging that our dogs were a bit of a nuisance to passing cars, we and the other owners felt that their virtues were too sterling for us to have them put down on that account.

The one person who came to terms with Mot's habit, in a most satisfactory manner, was Elwyn, our next-door neighbour. At the time, his children were attending the primary school in the village, and this meant that he passed our farm four times a day in his Land-Rover, delivering and collecting them—and four times a day, as he paused at the turning, he was insultingly chased and barked at.

But one afternoon, on his way to pick the children up, a solution occurred to him. He had to wait a moment at the end of the lane for traffic to pass, and in that moment his eye was caught by a cap pistol that the children had left on the shelf above the dashboard. So, lowering his window, he leaned out, and, pointing it at the frantic dog, fired a short burst of several rounds about nine inches from his ear.

Mot was scandalised. He had never imagined anything like this, and when he hit the ground again, after leaping three feet into the air, he clapped his tail between his legs and bolted, as fast as he could lay legs to the ground. He never menaced the Land-Rover again.

It is the vehicle and not the individual that the dog chases, as we realised when we heard of another successful cure, this time effected by an acquaintance of ours who was a representative for an animal feeding-stuffs firm.

'I was living in a village then, and to get to the main road I had to go along a lane, and just at the same place, this damned dog always jumped out at me. So one day, I was ready for him—I opened the door, and just held it close with my hand, and then when he jumped out—wham! I pushed it open, and caught him full across the shoulder as I drove past. It knocked him on his back in the ditch, I can tell you. I looked in the mirror and

saw him slinking away, so I knew I hadn't actually *killed* him
... and he never went for me again!

'But the funny thing was, it only worked for that car. Seven
or eight months later, I got a new one, and he was just as bad
as ever ... '

'But didn't you do the same thing again, as it worked so well
the first time?'

'No—I moved, instead!'

Mot was always a working dog rather than a pet, and, as the
years went by, we found ourselves rather hankering for the sort
of dog that we had known in our respective childhoods—a dog
that lives in the house and identifies itself completely with the
family, usually developing a king-sized personality in the
process.

By this time we had become friendly with another farming
couple, called John and Ruth Spong, who lived a mile or two
away, and who, as well as owning a splendid herd of Friesian
cattle, bred dachshunds. Not just any old dachshunds, either.
These were aristocrats. They went to shows, and their prize
tickets lined the kitchen rafters and overflowed, a colourful
medley, into the dining-room. On three occasions, one of their
kennel had had the honour of being best of breed at Cruft's, and
their stud dog, Toby, had collected more challenge certificates
than any other representative of his breed before or since.

Of course, once you get into this dog business, you realise
that there are dachshunds *and* dachshunds. Of the various
possible kinds, John and Ruth kept three—standard smooths,
miniature smooths, and miniature wire-hairs, and it was in the
breeding of the last that they were particularly pre-eminent.

But non-dog-minded people like us did not have sufficient
expertise to recognise the particular virtues that made so many
of their dogs champions. We just knew that, when we went to
see Ruth and John, we were greeted by a fury of barking, and
then, when the kitchen door was opened, by a torrent of jolly,
furry little atomies that frisked over our shoes, and pressed,
wagging and grinning round us with the utmost sociability and
goodwill. Then, when you had forced your way into the house,
and were sitting round the table, individualities would begin
to assert themselves, as Ruth or John addressed one or other

of them by name. 'No, *not* on the table, Prika! that's right, settle down. And you can leave him alone, too, Sammy! *SHUT UP JUDY!*' and so on. Eventually, most of them would retire to their low wooden benches round the walls, and normal conversation—always very entertaining in that house—could be resumed, unless a scrap broke out between what Ruth called 'the middle-aged puppies', always more volatile than their elders.

It was one of the middle-aged puppies who decided to sell himself to Desmond. The first time we saw him, he barked a tremendous lot, even having to be picked up and shushed— when, after a few grumbling remarks into Ruth's neck, he admitted us, and turned on us his bright, glowing goblin glance, while he wagged his whip-like tail. When he was put down on the floor, he bustled up to Desmond in the most sociable way, and pushed a cold, shining nose into his hand. Desmond was taken with him.

The next time Desmond had occasion to visit the Spongs, Hunter singled him out again, and—most telling stroke! when Desmond rose to leave, who should he find sitting in the passenger seat of the van? Who else but Hunter? As flattery goes, it may have been corny, but it was certainly effective. Desmond was touched, and attracted by this little personality who seemed so bent on catching his eye; and the upshot of it was that, a week or two later, Hunter became ours, and took his place, as of right, on the passenger seat of the van beside Desmond.

We felt a certain anxiety about Mot's reaction to this small, hairy, bustling being that was to invade his home; but as it turned out we need not have worried. One of the nicest aspects of Mot's character turned out to be his gentle forbearance towards creatures smaller than himself. To be sure, Hunter was not aggressive. At the first introduction, he rolled over on his back in an attitude of the most abject submission, quivering with fear, and even urinating, childishly, as Mot's grave nose examined him. But both dogs soon learned that there was no need for suspicion or fear, and they became good friends and companions, within the limits imposed by their widely differing physiques.

This physical difference was their only problem. For when

they were let out in the morning and bounded off to play, it almost inevitably followed that Mot lost Hunter. In half a dozen bounds the big dog would be fifty yards across the field, and then, swinging round with his big grin, he would find himself face to face with—nothing! While Hunter, six yards in from the gate, doggedly pursued him ascending and descending each tump of grass like a determined mountaineer assaulting the Matterhorn. If Mot did see his friend, beetle-like, on the horizon, and dash back to frisk with him, it was a hundred pounds to a pinch of snuff that he would bowl Hunter over in his exuberance. But Hunter never minded. He had the big heart that is often found in a diminutive body, and he would roll straight over again, busy little legs scrabbling madly as he came upright, in his eagerness to get on with the chase.

Hunter really was all big heart in spite of his smallness, and sometimes this quality of his became quite a nuisance. We were taking the cows up the lane one morning after milking, and suddenly it was as if they had come to an invisible barrier. In spite of us, and Mot, walking behind them, they all stopped, abruptly. Then they turned, and, almost apologetically, began to try to come back past us in the opposite direction. It was Hunter, of course. What idea he had in his mind I can't imagine, but there he was—planted squarely in the middle of the lane, growling briskly, and pitting his twelve pounds of body-weight entirely successfully against approximately twenty-five tons of assorted Friesians. When called away by Desmond, who had to go round the impasse through an adjacent field, he came at once, and quite willingly, clearly considering his duty done. We felt that his name might almost be changed to Horatio.

His full pedigree name was something of a gentle joke, suitable for a 'mini-wire', which Ruth always tells me are the clowns of the dachshund world. He rejoiced in the lofty cognomen of 'Peredur Mighty Hunter'; his brother was P. Mighty Warrior—and their father, a dog I never met, was Mighty Thunderer.

But it was not only the mini-wires that were characters. One evening we were at the Spongs' house for a party, and the senior standard smooth stud dog was admitted to be one of our number. He was a benevolent fellow called Paprika, a red-coated dog, of full age, but with a marvellous social manner. Nearly all of us who were present had at least a bowing acquaintance with him, and he went the rounds in the most urbane manner, having a word with everybody, and making us all welcome. But when we all moved into the dining-room and began to eat the delicious buffet supper we forgot him, and he, having done his social duty, clearly decided that now he was at liberty to attend to the needs of number one. So, ascending a handy chair, he addressed himself to a dish of cheese dip, and before anybody noticed it, he had eaten about a pound of it. The only bit of it he disliked was some finely-chopped celery, so he painstakingly sorted this out, and deposited the bits in a tidy little pyramid on the carpet beneath his chair . . . He was a dog with a good deal of savoir faire.

Paprika, or Priss, as he was known to his intimates, was the grandfather of my little dog, the next we had from the Spongs, a dog who was ordered before she was even born. I wanted a dog of my own, and there were several definite qualities I wanted it to have. It had to be short-coated, for one thing. Perhaps because of my childhood obsession with horses, I have always loved a silky, glossy coat in an animal, and Mot and Hunter were both rough. Then, remembering Folly, it had to be sheep-proof. In this matter, a dachshund particularly recommended itself. With such short legs, surely it could not keep up with a determined sheep? And finally, my ideal animal had to be black-and-tan, with eyebrow and muzzle markings to give distinction and prettiness to the face. So a standard smooth dachshund seemed the obvious answer, and when I heard that one of the bitches of that ilk was pregnant, I put my name down for a puppy, always assuming that there was at least one black-and-tan bitch in the litter.

There was; and having had her booked from the moment she was conceived, I was allowed to choose her name. So I opted for Peredur Siskin—and it is to my choice, and to Ruth and John's passion for consistency, that the owners of Peredur Serin, Sanderling, and Starling are indebted for their dogs' names.

Siskin was a charming little creature. She was still quite a puppy when we fetched her home, which was something new, for both Mot and Hunter had been six months old when we had

127

had them. So we had the pleasure of her baby softness—her ridiculous gambols—her miniature growls and squeaks as she played tug-of-war with our slippers—and her sudden collapses into sleep, in charming, puppyish attitudes, when she had played herself out.

But it was after Siskin had grown up that our dogs had their worst adventure, and she, of the three of them, was the one who came nearest to disaster in the course of it.

It started curiously enough. It was in January, and a savage black frost had settled on the land, binding the pastures in a grip of iron and making the warm kitchen a particularly welcome haven when the day's work was done. Both dachshunds were sleeping in front of the Aga one evening when, hearing a scratch at the door, I rose to open it, and Mot tottered in. At first I could not think what on earth was the matter with him, for to all appearances he was in exactly the same state as a homecoming sailor who has spent an evening pub-crawling, and now presents himself, rather the worse for wear, back at his ship. I had never heard of a dog going out and getting itself drunk, but that was what it looked like—and as he reeled, grinned foolishly, fell over, wagged his tail in great loopy circles, and bumped into the furniture, I almost felt like smelling his breath to see if it could possibly be true. I thought and thought, but could think of nowhere he could possibly have picked up any intoxicants, but there he was—obviously as drunk as a lord.

We had been to enough hairy parties in our unregenerate youth to be well aware that sleep is the sovereign remedy for alcohol, so we decided to do nothing about Mot's lapse until we saw how he was in the morning. And though he stretched himself out by the Aga and snored like any old drunken reprobate, in the morning he was all right again. So we did nothing.

Two nights later, both the male dogs came in reeling and hiccoughing and keeled over on the rug—but, again by morning they had slept it off, and though puzzled, we didn't feel that it was anything worse than curious. Hunter, in particular, was a riot as a drunk, and almost seemed to appreciate the audience reaction that his reelings, rollings, and fainting in coils, produced. But we still couldn't think what they could possibly be getting that was having this extraordinary effect on them.

A few nights later all three dogs came in drunk, and, saying to one another, 'I suppose they'll sleep it off again,' we arranged them on the mat by the Aga, and took ourselves off to bed. But though Mot and Hunter were awake and normal next morning, Siskin was still comatose, and as limp as a rag doll. So we rang up the vet.

It was one of Mr. Harries's assistants, a Mr. Williams, who came out to see her, and he had to confess himself puzzled. 'She's obviously picked up some kind of poison,' he said, 'but nothing I can think of quite seems to fit the symptoms. Organo-chlorines—organo-phosphoruses—no, not quite right— Have you had the rat men round recently?' But we hadn't, and Siskin wasn't the sort of dog to go roaming and pick up something on someone else's farm.

Mr. Williams told us that the main danger was pneumonia, and that we should have to sit up with her, and turn her over onto her other side at least once an hour. He gave her an injection, and asked us to ring him in the morning, to report progress. Then he drove away in his Land-Rover, amid the first blinding flurries of snow.

I took first stint as a night nurse with Siskin. We moved her into the sitting-room, and laid her in front of the anthracite stove, in a carefully constructed niche of propped up screens and boxes, to keep any whisper of a draught off her. For myself, I pulled two armchairs together, and, setting the alarm clock for one o'clock, I settled down to snatch what sleep I could in my clothes, and with the light on. Everyone who has sat up with a patient will recall the physical discomfort of these night vigils —how your eyes itch, and your tongue feels too big for your mouth; how you drag your legs up to fit into your improvised shakedown, and curl up with all the tight bits of your clothes cutting into you—and how you lie, aching and cramped, and certain you won't catch a wink of sleep, until crash! the brazen alarm right by your ear jerks you out of an uneasy doze, and you get up to perform your seemingly hopeless chores for the patient yet again.

Conscientiously, I turned Siskin every hour, sponged her

129

dry lips, and tried to trickle a drop of water down her throat. She just swallowed, vaguely, but that was all. Otherwise she lay still, eyes shut, breathing slowly, unconscious of all that went on around her.

There was deep snow on the ground when I drew back the curtains as the next morning limped in after my broken night. Two feet of feathery purity lay on the yard and the garden, but already the council snowploughs and gritting lorries were making brown channels up the main road, for the milk collection lorries to get round on their vital journeys. Heavy-eyed, I made the tea and woke Desmond, and together we went out through the snow to begin the milking.

Mr. Williams was even more puzzled when I rang him up to say that Siskin's condition was unchanged. 'I'd like some of the other vets in the firm to have a look at her,' he said. 'Wrap her up very warmly, and bring her into the surgery this morning, and perhaps one of them will be able to recognise what's the matter with her.' But, when they had her on the table, the four of them clustered round and examined her without any enlightenment. Until a chance word gave us the clue. For as one of them straightened himself up after listening to her heartbeat, and remarked, 'It's as if she's in a state of very deep anaesthesia,' Desmond and Mr. Williams and I all looked at each other and realised in a flash what the trouble must be.

For Mr. Williams had been on the farm about a fortnight previously, delivering a badly impacted calf. And, when he did manage to get it away, it was damaged and had to be destroyed. And the way a vet destroys a newborn calf is to inject a massive shot of nembutal direct into its heart. And of course, the weather being iron-hard, there was no way of burying the little creature, so it had been put away behind the buildings to await the return of softer circumstances, and there the dogs had obviously been going for a bit of illicit feasting between meals. Mot and Hunter must have eaten just enough to affect them a little bit, and make them look drunk, but Siskin presumably had eaten the heart itself, where the full concentration of the drug still rested. It very nearly killed her.

Very nearly—but not quite. For when Desmond was doing his stint of nursing that night, he was awakened from his uneasy

130

slumbers by a weak turmoil in Siskin's box, between two and three in the morning. 'Oh! God! she's in her death throes!' he thought, hastening over to her, with thoughts of the dead hours of the night when souls are on a loose chain crowding in on him. But it wasn't death—it was life, and what Siskin was trying to do was to reach a bowl of warm milk he'd been trying to spoon into her earlier, and which had been put down, in her sight-line, on the corner of the hearth. When he brought it to her she managed to sit up long enough to lap it all up, and then, turning over under her own power for the first time in fifty hours, she went to sleep again. Her improvement continued and at seven in the morning she climbed groggily out of her sick bed, which had clearly become very distasteful to her, and went to lie, in a more normal manner, on the hearth rug. It took a stiff course of antibiotics to clear up the last traces of the pneumonia, and for a day or two Mr. Williams still thought it was touch and go—but in our eyes that bowl of milk was the turning-point, from which she seemed to get better and better all the time.

Poor little Siskin did not live to be old, though. When she was about five, she developed nephritis, and, in spite of treatment, lost weight until she was no better than a skeleton. It was so wretched to see her sad-eyed and listless, lying about in the yard instead of playing with the other dogs as she had been used to. Presumably, her kidneys not functioning as they should, she must have felt headachy and unwell all the time. So, in the end, we decided that it was kinder to put her to sleep than to let her die by inches, and one sunny day the merciful injection was given, and she fell asleep very quietly with her head in my hand. We buried her by the camellia in the garden, glad, at least, that we had been able to spare her the last of her illness's sufferings.

Hunter died unfortunately too. He rushed onto the road one morning when the dogs were let out of their shed, and went right under the wheels of two cars, in an overtaking situation, which were roaring up the hill side by side. He was killed outright, and he lies under the cherry tree, which is his memorial.

II

When I was a child, I was horse-mad, even to the extent of wanting to be a horse myself. I thought they were the most wonderful and beautiful of animals, and imitated them in every way that I could, considering anatomical limitations. I would be aware of the bit on the corners of my mouth, the straps of the bridle on my cheeks, the subtle pressure of my rider's legs guiding me round corners, or accelerating me to an illicit gallop along the school corridors—and I responded with suitable snortings, shyings, and curvettings. I always saw myself as very spirited. The mistresses got a good deal of quiet fun out of my silly antics, and the English mistress coined a nickname for me that won a good deal of applause in the Staff Room—the Hippophile.

My hippophilia declined with the years to more reasonable proportions, but there was still enough of it left when we bought our farm to make me feel that here was a grand opportunity to get a horse of my own at last, or rather a pony.

The first one I had was bought from a neighbour of Dai's father, called Byron. Byron is a great big man, and when he was called up to do his national service they took one look at his great frame and put him into the Coldstream Guards, where he eventually became a sergeant. When we first knew him, he was the tenant of a farm called Oer Nant Fawr, which means Big Cold Stream—rather a curious coincidence. Byron is another hippophile, and always had a few ponies on his place, either breeding mares, or young ones that he was breaking in. Quite often he would ride one of these young ones round by our farm, and stop for a chat, and for me to admire the current pupil.

One of the ones he brought round was a little black mare, a three-year-old, rather an ugly little creature really, but full of energy. She had a plain head, and a curious long light body, but her legs were clean and sound, and she moved well and looked as if she enjoyed her work. We decided to make him an offer for her.

Doing a deal with Byron is never a straightforward matter of handing over the cash and getting an object in return. He loves a deal so much that he never lets it be concluded until all possible permutations of barter and cash have been explored, and as Desmond is like this too, both parties, through previous deals, are well provided with material for the game.

'Well, what I want for her is eighty, but say you were to take that old Dai Brown tractor that's on the top field by the house and make it a hundred, that'd be putting her in at seventy-five, because that tractor's a gift at twenty-five . . . '

'I don't want the Dai Brown, but if you've got some hay to spare I might . . . '

'Or what about sixty-five, say, and you throw in a couple of dozen hens and a chick drinker . . . '

'What if I took the two ponies, the black one and the little registered Welsh mare and you could have some of it in eggs . . . '

And so on and so forth. I can't remember the final deal, but as well as money, and the pony, it involved hens and eggs on our side, and baled hay and a roll of sheep-netting on his. It was finally concluded to everyone's satisfaction, and when all the loose ends had been tidied up, Byron delivered the pony in his trailer.

How proud I felt of her, as she stepped down the ramp, and walked into her new home, ears pricked enquiringly, sharp dark eyes glancing around, taking everything in. We had put a gate across the old stable to make a box for her, as she had been kept in all winter, and it was only February, and too cold to turn her out. She was not clipped, but the weather was dank and sometimes freezing, and we felt that she would be better in.

Next morning, as soon as I could be spared from the milking, I went in to the stable to see to her in a state of considerable euphoria. I filled her hay rack and water bucket, and tied her up to the manger while I forked over her bedding and sorted the manure and the soiled straw from the clean. Then I fetched my grooming tools—saved up for out of Christmas and birthday presents in the hippophiliac days, and carefully cherished ever since—and cleaned her down. I brushed her all over with the body brush, scraping it over the curry comb every now and again to clean it, and brushed out the coarse, blue-black mane and tail with the dandy brush. She was good and compliant, pulling her sweet hay from the rack, and moving to and fro as I directed her. I felt I could not admire her enough, from the sooty velvet of her muzzle to her neat black heels, where the little curl on each fetlock finished off the leg so charmingly.

After breakfast I saddled and bridled her, and took her out for a ride. We met a milk lorry or two in the narrow lanes, which made her sidle and sweat, but each time I managed to edge her into a deep gateway while the monster passed, and I hoped she would soon get used to them. Some heifers behind a hedge gave us a few anxious moments, as they rushed up and down, hidden from us, bellowing. The pony drew up trembling; then, wrenching her ears to and fro, she tried to whip round, but I was able to prevent her, and she soon settled down. We were out for about an hour and a half, and I was pleased with her as I led her back into her box.

I took her out for the same kind of ride again the following afternoon, but this time fate was not so kind. There were no milk lorries, and we were proceeding placidly enough up a steep hill when suddenly, round a corner, we came face to face with the school bus. And this time I was not alert enough to stop the sudden halt, half-rear, and whip-round that is a nervous horse's instinctive reaction to danger. A good rider would have anticipated it and taken the appropriate blocking measures in time, but my reactions were too slow. And so it was that I found myself hurtling at the speed of light down a very steep hill on a tarmac road, the pony slithering all over the road, striking sparks from her shoes, and the bus-driver, like a fool, following us down, thereby increasing her panic, instead of waiting, stationary, until I could get control of her again. It was a nasty moment. I always find in such a situation that my imagination works at double speed, and as I frantically wrestled with the reins I saw her down on the road, with her knees cut to ribbons—or slithering over on her side, with me underneath her, my leg broken—I heard, in my mind, the scrape of her slipping hooves, the grunt as she hit the road, the crack of my bone splitting—and then, as I fought to control her, the cheek-strap of the bridle broke, and the bit nearly came out of her mouth.

By the grace of God, just in front of us was the entrance to
134

a farmyard, and the gate was open. So desperately lunging forward, I seized the actual ring of the snaffle and dragged her head round—and luckily her body followed it, and there we were, safe in somebody's farm-yard, sweating and trembling, while the bus, with its load of goggle-eyed children, swept past us and out of sight. I mended the bridle with a bit of string and endured a jumpy ride home, with great shyings at every motor vehicle that passed.

The next day we were busy. After lunch, I said to Desmond, 'I must take that pony out—she'll be jumping out of her skin. I'll try to spare an hour, and give her some jogging along the road.' But Desmond pointed out that there wasn't really an hour to spare, and suggested taking her out in our own fields for a shorter, sharper bout of exercise. 'Give her a good gallop for about twenty minutes,' he said, 'surely that'll do as well for today?' And though I knew it was wrong, really, I assented. We were very short of time.

What followed was inevitable. I had ridden round two big fields, first at a trot, then at a jerky sort of canter—the mare, very full of herself, snatching at the bit and throwing her head around all the time—and, thinking I had her well enough in hand, I took her down into the dip field, intending to canter down the gentle slope, and take a bit of the ginger out of her galloping up the far side, which was steep. Alas for my over-confidence! For, feeling me urge her forward, she went mad with excitement, and plunging her head between her knees set off downhill at full gallop, bucking like a lunatic. And that was that. At the third buck, I was propelled off her back like a bullet, landed on my left knee at high speed, and lay there, watching her disappearing into the distance, still flourishing her heels, while I palpated my knee and wondered if I would ever walk again. I did, of course—within about two minutes. My knee wasn't broken, but it was agony for two or three weeks, and I felt in no hurry to resume my riding. The pony had to be turned out to get her exercise by herself, which she did in the most spirited way, scouring about like a chamois, galloping easily up the most precipitous slopes, and setting the echoes ringing with her prodigious snorts. When the weather improved, we turned her out altogether, and she became rather a nuisance, jumping the electric fence and chasing the cows around for entertainment. I did not much want to ride her, so I made excuses not to, until eventually it became obvious that it was pointless to keep her, and we decided to take her to a sale.

There is a monthly horse sale not far from here, in the small Cardigan market town of Llanybyther. (A difficult one to pronounce—say Thlan-ee-*buther*, the last th soft as in 'bother'.) Other creatures are auctioned there, of course, at more frequent intervals, but 'Llanybyther' is synonymous with horse sales, and if you asked anyone, 'What were the prices like at Llanybyther last week?' you would be taken flat aback if he discoursed on the money that had changed hands for fat sheep or weaner pigs.

So we entered our mare for Llanybyther, and engaged the good offices of Byron both to take her up in his trailer and to stiffen our resolve with his much greater experience of horse-dealing.

As the day of the sale approached, we groomed the mare up, and got her newly shod. She had got her summer coat by now, and it gleamed, midnight-black, but her mane and tail still looked rough and untidy. I thought about pulling them—but shrank from it in the end. I knew how it was done, but had never actually tried it, and I thought in my ignorance I might make her look worse rather than better. In the end, I plaited her mane up on the morning of the sale, and although the plaits were rather untidy and bunchy, they did stay in, and gave her a certain air of smartness which went well with her rather jaunty carriage.

Unfortunately Desmond could not manage to come to the sale, but with Byron and Glenys his wife I felt we were fielding quite a strong team, and the three of us crowded into the Land-Rover and set off to Llanybyther with quite high hopes.

You could easily see what kind of a market you were going to as you got nearer to the town. Every second vehicle on the road was pulling a trailer, over the tailboard of which you could sometimes see a blanketed, tail-bandaged form, or sometimes, if the occupant was a small pony, just a pair of little sharp ears. When we got within a mile, the traffic stream was augmented by led and ridden horses and ponies, in such numbers that you might have thought that every animal in West Wales was converging on Llanybyther to be sold that day.

We pulled into the crowded saleground, and, with difficulty, found a place to park. Then we let down the ramp, and fetched the nervous, sweating mare out of the box. It was not surprising that she felt anxious; the confusion was tremendous. All around was the rumble and thump of ramps being lowered and animals clattering down them—lorry engines growled, horses and ponies neighed, and a bevy of donkeys in one corner kept up a hideous, continuous braying.

Byron was in his element. Almost at once a little old man sidled over to our pony, felt her legs and looked into her mouth. 'How much, boss?' he asked; but when Byron said, 'A hundred and twenty,' he spat on the ground, expressively, and wandered away. We tied her to the trailer, and rubbed some of the sweat off her, then took it in turns to stay with her while the others wandered around, looking at the rest of the talent, and admiring the goods displayed for sale on stalls near the entrance. There were saddlers, veterinary chemists, stalls selling models of horses in brass and china, and one enterprising artist, who, as well as selling his brilliantly-coloured horse pictures, was taking commissions for equine portraits in pastels. I bought a yellow tail bandage and a smart new white webbing halter, and, with these on her, the mare did begin to look rather neat. Several people looked her over, but there was no very obvious interest, and we began to wonder if our asking price was possibly a bit unrealistic. 'Put the saddle on and ride her round a bit,' advised Byron. 'That way more people will get a look at her—we're a bit out of the way here.' So I did. I had not been on her back since the last time I fell off it, and I did feel a certain pang of fear as I climbed aboard; but in spite of the traffic and the hubbub, she was as good as gold. We had one little barney when she tried to refuse to pass a cattle lorry creeping slowly along the road, but I had a stick in my hand this time, and eventually she gave in and went on in the way I directed her. I took her round several times, through the parked lorries, out into the road, back round the front of the market where the stallion-owners paraded their

137

beasts in the hope of picking up stud bookings, and down past the ring where the selling was already in progress. There was a dense crowd of people round the railings, but from my seat on the mare's back, I could see well enough, and I stopped and watched for a while. The 'ring' itself was not circular, but was a rectangle of concrete about twenty-five yards long, down which the horses were trotted, either in hand, or with a rider on their backs. A little man in a long coat—a dealer from the look of him—had stationed himself about half-way down, and as each horse passed him he cracked his whip viciously just behind its hocks. Naturally enough, most of the horses swerved and shied at this, slipping on the concrete, and several of the riders were nearly unseated, but nobody seemed to complain. I viewed with gloom my own probable performance in these conditions, and thanked heaven that we were near the end of the catalogue. Perhaps he would have gone by the time we came in.

But, as morning changed to afternoon, being at the end of the catalogue began to seem less of an advantage—indeed, as time went on, I really began to wonder if we should succeed in selling her at all. Several hundred animals had changed hands in the two rings, and the crowds seemed to be thinning. Prices were definitely lower than they had been in the morning. Were we going to have to give her away, or even take her back again, unsold? We began to feel anxious.

Then, as I rode round my circuit, I was flagged down by a horsey-looking man with a very red face. He had clearly been drinking. 'Run her up there, Miss!' he cried, indicating a stretch of road, so I trotted her away, and then back towards him again, and then held her while he looked at her teeth and felt her legs.

'How much d'you want?' I tried £115. 'Too much, too much —but look here! I'm going back up North with a load of horses now, and I just want one more to fill up my lorry—what about £110? Not that she's really worth it, but still . . . ' I was happy enough with that actually, but I felt it would be too unfarmerish to give in without a struggle, and the upshot of it was, after several more minutes of bargaining, that he gave me a cheque for £112, and I gave him the pony, the new halter, and £1 in luck money. For some reason or other, I kept the tail bandage.

I felt substantial qualms as I pocketed the cheque and walked back, with my saddle, bridle and tail bandage, to tell Byron and Glenys what I had done. After all, his cheque might bounce, and I didn't know him from Adam. But I decided to risk it in the end because his horse-lorry, with the address on it, looked so exceedingly prosperous, and in the event I need not have worried. The cheque went through perfectly all right, and, indeed, when I happened to see him a year or so later, he remembered me and the pony, and told me spontaneously about the people he had eventually sold her to, who sounded very nice.

After the black pony we had a lapse of some time without any horses on the place, and it was through Byron again that we once more entered the lists. It started one day in June, when, exercising past the farm on a rough bay gelding he was breaking in, Byron said, 'I wish you'd come up and have a look at the colt my cream mare's just had, Elizabeth. The stallion was an Arab, and the colt's a winner. You should just see his action!' So that evening Desmond and I drove up, and there in the field was this charming creature, three days old, red bay in colour, who cavorted about after his mother, or made little solo sorties onto the buttercups on his long thin legs like a spirited spider. I adored him.

But I didn't really think of buying him until six months later, when Byron pulled up outside the garden with his Land-Rover and trailer, early one morning, as I was pegging out some tea-towels.

'What are you taking where?' I asked him.

'It's the colt—I'm taking him to Llanybyther. But it's a rotten trade, they say.'

'What are you hoping for?'

'Well, I'll be lucky if I get twenty, twenty-one, I suppose.'

'If that's all you're offered, bring him back here, and I'll give you £22 for him' I said on impulse.

And in due course, on the evening of the same day, I found myself the owner of a newly-weaned Arab-Welsh colt foal who looked like making fourteen hands when he was full grown.

139

I put him in a box for the night, and he promptly jumped out, so I had to fasten up the top half of the door. In the end, to keep him company, we bought another pony from Byron, a small one for the children, called Olivia, and the two of them settled down very well together.

I didn't think of a name for my new colt for a few days, but then the man came to service my washing machine, and I saw from his worksheet that his name was Mr. Rook. This seemed to strike exactly the right note, so Rook my little lad became, although we all tended to soften it down to 'Rookie-boy'—he was so sweet.

Rook was always accustomed to being handled. Byron halter-broke him at a very early age, and taught him to allow his feet to be picked up, and I continued the treatment, which saved a lot of trouble later. He was never at all difficult to catch—rather the opposite, indeed—for when you went into his field he was so glad to see you that he would hasten over with cries of joy, pulling up in front of you with great slippings and slidings and sittings-back on his haunches. I knew he meant no harm, but the children didn't care for it at all and would disappear with wails of terror behind my back as he thundered up. Olivia, on the other hand, sometimes played hard to get, and bumbled determinedly off in another direction when one went to catch her. We cured this in the time-honoured way by catching her to feed her. We left a head-collar on her when we turned her out—then we visited her several times in the course of a day, with a small handful of cattle cake in a scoop, which we offered her. At first she was leery and suspicious, thinking she was going to be caught—but she could smell the cake, and presently greed overcame discretion, and she poked her nose into the scoop. You could see that every nerve was on edge even as she was eating—one move of your hand towards her head-collar, and she would have been off like the wind. But as nothing happened, and we forbore to touch her, her confidence increased. When she was eating freely from the scoop, I began to take hold of the head-collar, but as soon as she had finished, I let her go immediately, which of course she didn't mind. The last stage in the process was catching her and leading her out of the field—but, instead of saddling her, simply taking her into the stable for another little feed of nuts. After a fortnight or so of this, she would come up to you as you went into the field, practically begging to be caught, and we never had any more trouble with her in that way.

The trouble we did have with her was health trouble, and in the end it proved to be terminal. It began one cold day in late November, when she and Rook were grazing across the road in Parc y Mynnydd. Dai was with us then, and he came in during the morning, saying, 'There's something the matter with the Welsh mare, she's standing all hunched up.' It was true. There she was, huddled under the hedge, obviously very unwell, and when we tried to bring her up to the stable, she obviously found it hard to move. She tottered and nearly fell and, as soon as she was in the box, resumed her awkward position, with arched back, and head hanging by her knees.

The vet didn't find her trouble hard to diagnose. 'Ragwort,' he said, succinctly. 'These mountain ponies often get this sort of trouble. When times are hard during the winter, on the mountain, they eat anything they can find, including ragwort. And, of course, it's poisonous. The trouble is, the poison is cumulative, and builds up gradually in the liver. Then any little thing —a slight chill, perhaps—precipitates the liver collapse, and you get this acute condition developing. Look how jaundiced she is, poor little thing.' And, turning back her eyelid, he showed us the yellow stain, plain to be seen, on the white of her eyeball.

Olivia recovered more or less from her bout of jaundice, but she was never really herself again, and eventually we gave her back to Byron. He kept her for a year or two, but none of us was really surprised when she was found dead in her field one morning. It was a sad end. The trouble about a disease like hers is that liver tissue apparently cannot to any extent regenerate, so any damage done remains as a permanent handicap to the animal.

Rook, however, who had never known what it was to scratch around for food on a bare mountain, continued to thrive. In his second summer he gave up being a bay and decided to be a roan, a sort of purple roan, something between a blue and a strawberry. His mane and tail and his points were black, and

141

with his two little white hind socks he looked very stylish in his new coat. When winter came and he got furry, he reverted to a dark reddish bay colour.

Whether it was as a result of running with a mare or whether he was just sexually precocious I don't know, but long before he was one year old, Rook began to demonstrate awareness of his stallionhood. He often tried to mount Olivia, but she parried his advances with kicks and squeals, and he was fairly easily discouraged. But to us he became constantly meaner and more tiresome in every way. He took to biting for one thing. This was not as a result of too much tit-bit-feeding for, being aware of this danger, I had made a point of never offering him delicacies, so he never learned to expect them. It seemed just chauvinist male piggery, and you had to learn to look after yourself. It was when he was on the halter that he was most persistently snappy, and the only answer was to keep your right hand right up to his face on the halter rope, so that he couldn't do more than try to gnaw you at close range, which was easily enough circumvented. We knew his personality would change when he was gelded, so we didn't worry unduly, but there was one occasion when his upsurgent manhood nearly landed him and me under the wheels of a car.

It happened in March, when he was about nine months old. I was taking him across the road to turn him into Parc y Mynnydd, and he was being his usual disagreeable self, trying to nip my hand, and surging over onto my side of the road all the time, so that he nearly trod on my toes at every step. But I had made him do more or less what I wanted, and we arrived at the field gate bloody but unbowed. The devil, however, was waiting his chance, and as I took one hand off the halter rope to open the gate, he put a new idea into Rook's head, and sat back to await events. And he didn't have to wait long for Rook suddenly reared right up, pulling the halter rope through my hand, and struck at me savagely from up there, with his front feet. This was unexpected, but not fatal—but unfortunately, in drawing his off fore foot down the front of my donkey jacket, he stuck it into my pocket, and couldn't get it out. And there we were, like a couple of ill-assorted dancing partners, charlestoning about on the main road—I with the halter still in my hand, he on three legs with one foot in my pocket, and a car swinging up the hill at forty miles an hour, obviously hoping to make the gradient without having to change down. Everything happened very quickly then. The car swerved, with a blast on the horn—Rook lunged violently, and tore his foot away with my pocket and the front of my coat still on it. And I let go of the halter and sat down with a bump on the road, following my charleston with a black bottom in dead earnest. The car disappeared towards Carmarthen, and Rook towards Meidrim, shedding his foot-cosy on the way. But luckily he did not get very far. Another car, coming up more temperately, turned him, and he galloped back again, and through the field gate which I had by now had time to open for him.

I was anxious to get him gelded as soon as possible, but the vet told me to wait for the weather to warm up first, and it was May before he thought it safe to perform the operation. Rook was then eleven months old.

We had him in the stable on the appointed day, and the first treatment meted out to him when the two vets arrived was a tranquillising injection. 'It'll work in a few minutes,' said Mr. Harries, the vet 'so take him out into the field now, while we get the thing ready. We prefer to castrate out of doors if it's possible—there's less risk of infection.'

Rook's dose had begun to affect him before the vets came into the field, festooned with coils of rope, and laden with boxes of equipment. He stood very quietly, with his eyes half-shut, sagging at the knees, and when they began to construct a complicated cat's cradle of rope around him, he neither stirred nor tried to bite them. Indeed, he didn't even seem to notice. Then when everything was ready, and Mr. Harries stood back and pulled a long end of the rope, he just folded up like a collapsing house of cards, and went down on his side in one movement.

'Good! That's right! sit on his head now!' cried Mr. Harries, bustling forward, and the grisly business began.

Country people are no less avid for spectacle than their city counterparts, and, swiftly though the vets worked, a crowd of six people and three dogs had hastened severally across the field before they finished, to watch the operation, to regale us with anecdotes of other castrations they had attended, or to growl and squabble over the disjecta membra, according to their kind.

'All right—let him get up then!' said Mr. Harries, a few minutes later 'and then you can put him back in the other field with his girl-friend if you want to!' So we took the ropes off Rook and encouraged him to struggle to his feet. Then we led him—still too drunk to attempt to bite—to Olivia's field, where he instantly tried, in a hazy sort of way, to mount her.

It took about a fortnight after the castration for Rook's stallionish characteristics to fade, and then he became a most agreeable animal. Gone were the biting, the striking, the barging about; instead, he became docile and amiable, growing in grace as much as in stature.

I left him until he was four before having him broken in. This job was done through a typically Welsh series of interlocking contacts, by a churn-lorry driver recommended to us. He was Aunty's-cousin's-husband's-sister's boy-friend to somebody in Meidrim—and very well he did it too. He brought him back, green but perfectly quiet, within three weeks, saying that he had been able to give his young children rides on him from the third day onwards! There is no doubt that constant handling makes a pony much easier to break in. Long before he was sent away for his formal breaking, Rook had been accustomed to being led, both at a walk and at a run—to being tied up—to being groomed all over—to having his feet picked up, and tapped (to get him ready for the smith's attentions), and to having a rope put round his belly, so that the feel of the girth should not be strange to him. I had also often leant across his back for a few seconds, with my feet off the floor, to accustom him to the sensation of bearing weight. I think he had come to the conclusion that human beings were a daft, fanciful lot, but harmless—so there was really nothing in the actual business of backing and mouthing to worry him.

The only difficulty we had with Rook after his breaking in was with his figure. We were tremendously busy that summer, having no regular help on the farm, and even though he lived on the barest grazing we could provide, he simply swelled and swelled. I never seemed to have two consecutive hours at a time to catch him, clean him, ride him, cool him, and turn him out; and in the end I decided it was a shame to keep him, when his youth and charm could be at someone else's disposal, who might make better use of it. So we took him to Llanybyther.

It was rather the same as the trip with the black mare, except that Desmond and I took him ourselves, in Elwyn's Land-Rover and trailer, and this time we had a stall in the covered part of the market, instead of having to camp out among the parked vehicles. Again, I rode him around—the saddle slipping continually on his rolls of fat—again horsey-looking people looked into his mouth, and ran their hands down his clean black legs; I felt quite proud of him. Apart from being fat, he was looking rather splendid. He was in his roan summer manifestation and, against his pinkish body, his black points gleamed jettily. His tail was a bit of a drawback, for he had managed to fill it with burdocks, and in trying to get them out, I had cut out rather a lot of hair—but his mane, in compensation, hung full and silky over his neck between his ears. He was rather excited by the bustle, and the crowd of strange horses and ponies, and neighed piercingly several times in his stall. We felt that he was making us a little conspicuous, but perhaps he was just being his own town crier. He was bought by a young man who owned a riding school, and I should think he would suit the job very well, for he had grown into an extremely strong pony, just about fourteen hands.

We have not had any other ponies since Rook and Olivia, but I have not sold any of my tack. You never know when an irresistible opportunity may crop up, and if one does, I want to be ready.

III

One of the consequences of having changed our farming, as I described in my first book *Buttercups and Daisy*, from milking cows to a suckler herd, is that we don't see the vets so much. While this is in some ways a good thing, and certainly saves a lot of money, we do rather miss them. We have always been very lucky in our vets, who have been entertaining as well as competent. Too entertaining, one of them remarked bitterly, once. One of our Ayrshire cows, Comfrey, had fallen ill with the highly dangerous condition of hypomagnesaemia—a metabolic disorder whose first symptom is often simply death. Luckily for us, Comfrey had it mildly, and we were able to drive her into the cowshed and tie her up to await the intravenous injection of magnesium that would put her out of danger. But one of the side-effects of hypomagnesaemia is that it makes the animal terribly bad-tempered, and while the vet was trying to raise a vein in her neck to inject into Comfrey—normally the most self-effacing of creatures—she suddenly became enraged. With a great echoing bull-like bellow she stuck her tongue out and attacked him. She couldn't get far, because she was chained up, but even so I never saw a man move so fast. Desmond and I, secure in the privileged spectator area of the hay-passage, fell around. 'You can laugh!' he said cynically, as he picked himself up and dusted himself off. 'Now come in here and grab hold of her nose!'

Our present firm of vets consists of Bill Jones, his wife, Martha, and their partner, Oliver. Bill has looked at so many sick animals that he has an uncanny knack now of spotting the ones that aren't going to 'do'. 'I don't like it,' he will say, looking, perhaps, at some fairly prosperous-looking creature who appears to the eye of inexperience to be just slightly off-colour. 'No, I don't like it at all.' Ten to one he is right, and the animal turns out to be just starting with some dread disease for which there is no cure. If on the other hand, looking at some desperately sick-seeming beast, he says, 'She's not so bad!' you can relax. It'll be all right. We had some Friesian heifers once that got husk. This is a parasitic throat-worm which they ingest with the grass, which gives them a nasty cough and spoils their condition, or, in extreme cases, brings on a pneumonia which can kill them. The worm eggs are ingested during the whole grazing season, but the conditions of late summer and early autumn are particularly conducive to a heavy infestation, and young cattle often begin to shows the signs of an attack quite suddenly then. It was so with our heifers. From being apparently well one day, they all suddenly began to cough, and one, the smallest, went down with pneumonia. Of course we sent for the vet.

Bill came up, and looked first at the very sick one, which we had in a box by itself. 'Hm, hm, not very good,' he said. 'She *may* pull through. And what about the others?'

'We've got them all in the yard for you to look at,' we told him. 'And if you don't think they're going to do, for heaven's sake whisper it, so there'll be a chance God won't hear you.'

But all was well. He moved in among them, checking their respiration and so on—and then 'I'll give them all a shot for the husk,' he said 'and'—cupping his hands round his mouth, and shouting towards the clouds hurrying by overhead—'they're going to live!' And, of course, they did.

Martha, his wife, deals with large animal practice just as easily as the men do. It is an education to see her pick up the back foot of an eleven-hundredweight cow to seek for the cause of lameness—she makes nothing of it, just picks it up like a smith picks up a horse's foot, and that's all there is to it. I have only once tried to imitate her, and when I found myself instantly on my back in the dunging channel, I decided to let the cobbler stick to his last.

Martha was unlucky enough to be on duty for the nastiest calving we ever had on this farm. It was a heifer, a pedigree Friesian, one of our Atalantas, and she went into labour at about evening milking time. By half past eleven she had got as far as presenting two front feet, but there the operation stuck, and, try as we might, we could not move the calf any further.

You hesitate to call the vet out at half past eleven at night, but it was obvious that the heifer couldn't go through the night in that state, and we thought in any case that perhaps 11.30 was better than the small hours of the morning so we telephoned.

Martha came up straight away, remarking that Bill was away for a few days, and, attaching calving ropes to the calf's feet, pulled. We all pulled. We pulled like mad and nothing happened. The heifer groaned and strained and lay down, but still the calf remained, absolutely lodged fast.

'Is there another man you could get?' asked Martha. 'A neighbour, perhaps?' So we telephoned our ever-kind neighbour

Elwyn, and he came and added his weight to the ropes, but it was still to no avail.

'It's no good. I shall have to get it out in pieces,' declared Martha finally. 'It's dead anyway, with all this pulling around, and being squeezed so tightly against the pelvic bones'. She returned to the boot of her car, and came back with a curious instrument—a kind of long metal tube with a wire dangling from it. This, acting rather on the principle of a cheese wire, was used to saw the calf into pieces, and the tube, through which the wire passed, prevented the cow herself from being damaged as the wire was pulled to and fro.

But first the loose end had to be passed round the calf's body, and, ignoring the discomfort, Martha lay down on her stomach behind the prostrate cow and reached deep, deep inside her. You do what you can for your vet in the way of sprinkling straw and brushing away mess, but a difficult calving is always a dirty sort of business, and good vets soon acquire a stoical disregard for the unpleasant floors they have to stretch out on. Their minds, I suppose, are taken up with the job in hand. I admire this attitude, and think many people could absorb some of it to their advantage. Nothing is more limiting for a human being than to be always worrying about dirt. Lots of the more delightful things in life, gardening to painting, make you dirty—but what does it matter? It all comes off in the end.

It seemed a long time that Martha was groping inside the cow, and we waited in an anxious group, ready to do anything we could to help. But eventually she managed to pass the wire round the right bit, and emerged, grimly triumphant. Then, giving Elwyn the ends of the wires, she instructed him to begin sawing, slowly and steadily, while she guided the instrument at the correct angle. In five minutes, it was through, and the first section of the pathetic little beast lay before us on the wet concrete floor. The wire was passed round again, between the legs this time, and the hind quarters, in two sections, were gently eased away. The afterbirth came next, and then there was no more we could do but to tuck up the heifer for the night with plenty of straw, hay, and a bucket of water. It was now half past two.

The calf's liver was clearly visible in its dismembered body, and though the rest of the carcass was destined for dog food, I thought I would keep this for ourselves, as some sort of compensation for the loss we had suffered. Calves' liver is usually beyond our budget. But curiously enough, it was uneatable, being tough, and very bitter, although the bile sac was not burst. 'That's because it was never *used*,' said one old farmer to whom I mentioned the phenomenon. 'Now if that calf had ever had a chance to suck, and had used his liver to digest food even once, you'd have found it different. It would have sweetened it.' It could be true, I suppose. I didn't ask him how he knew.

Not surprisingly, the heifer was not too well after such a difficult parturition. A hard calving often damages a nerve which controls the movement of the back legs, and the mother may be partly paralysed for days, or even weeks. It was so with Atalanta. She lay on the floor in the cowshed, completely unable to rise to her feet. It was an awkward predicament, because Desmond had to go to London the next day to take his mother to hospital for a major operation, and even a small paralysed cow is a bit heavy for a woman to heave around on her own. But, as always, the Welsh good neighbour system came to our aid, and either Elwyn or Dai (who used to work for us, but who had left by this time) came down a couple of times a day to help me with her. She could get up onto her knees without any difficulty, but the big push with the back legs that completes the standing-up process was beyond her. So I would milk out the two teats that were uppermost as she lay in the shed, and then the two of us would encourage her to kneel up, and, using her tail as a handle, haul her bodily upright and prop her against the wall. Then Dai, or Elwyn, would get a shoulder under the hook of her hip, and take the weight of her, to stop her collapsing on top of me, while I hastily milked out the other two quarters; then we would let her gently down again, on the other side to the one she had been on before. Elwyn told me that he had had a cow in this condition for three weeks which had eventually made a perfect recovery. 'I used to take her for walks in the field to get a bit of use back into her legs,' he said. 'She was pretty paralysed

149

still, and often she'd stagger and go to fall over. But I used to be there behind her, holding her up by her tail, and we'd totter about for ten minutes or so like that. She came good in the end.'

Atalanta came good, too. In spite of her bad start, she milked very well as a heifer, and even better as a second calver, which was the last lactation we had her for.

This was not, of course, by any means the only time that Martha had to stretch herself out on the wet ground to deliver a calf, and a story has trickled through the grapevine of another famous occasion which took place quite soon after she came to the district.

The farmer in question was an import, a Scot—a man of ripe years and decided views, whose chief characteristic, as everyone agreed, was a stubborn determination to have his own way in everything. He had sent for the vet to calve a cow that was in trouble, and he was not entirely pleased when a strange car drew up on his yard, and out stepped this small, slight girl. He grumbled; she explained (which is true) that she was just as capable of calving a cow as any man vet, and as there was nothing else he could do, he subsided, and, muttering, led her to her patient. But here they had their first fight. The cow was in the covered yard, with all the other cows milling around and Martha said that it should be in a box on its own. They argued the toss for some time, but in the end the point went to Martha, and they began to shepherd the animal out. Luck was not on her side, however. Halfway between the covered yard and the box, the cow lay down, and no persuasion that any one of them could apply would bring her to her feet again. So Martha had to go into action there and then, in the open. And of course it was raining too.

With a final clashing of grim looks with the farmer, she lay down, and inserted her arm into the cow to find out what was impeding the birth. But, by ill chance, the cow had gone down on a sloping yard facing uphill, and, try as she might, Martha's rubber-booted feet could get no purchase on the running wet concrete. Withdrawing her arm, she remarked icily to the farmer, 'Can't you see that I keep slipping? If you'd put your foot there'—jabbing on angry fore-finger at the concrete—'I could set my feet against it, and get a bit of purchase. Then perhaps we might get something done.'

This was a new experience for the touchy, masterful Scot; nobody had ever spoken to him like that in his life. But she was the vet, and it was his cow lying there in the rain on its side—so, swallowing his resentment as best he could, he stamped his foot down in the spot indicated, braced himself against the wall and said, 'Poosh against that, then lassie!' thinking to himself, 'Aye, ye can poosh the wa' down too if ye've a mind to, ye wee baggage! Pu' your foot there, is it, forbye?'

Martha worked her arm deep into the cow, and felt around. There were two calves, small ones, and they were presenting badly. She felt a folded hock, and straightened it—only to find it linked with a foreleg of the other animal. They were thoroughly muddled up. She sighed, shifted her position to ease the ache in her shoulder, and soldiered on.

The farmer looked down on her with unwilling admiration as she concentrated on disentangling the two calves. 'Aye, ye're digging in well, my lassie,' he thought. 'Ye mind me of my old terrier bitch, the way ye went in there—a grand dog after a badger she was, too!'

It was not long before Martha had sorted out the two calves, and drawn them into the world, but the long labour had been too much for one of them, and it was dead. The living calf was carried round to lie in front of its mother, and when she had licked it a little it was carried into the box, where she eagerly followed it. Martha completed her work in a chilly silence.

Finally, she was ready to go. She wound down the window of her car. 'Perhaps you could call me a little earlier next time, Mr. X,' she said crisply. 'Then I might have the pleasure of getting two *live* calves out for you.' But Mr. X was not mollified. 'Lassie, there wi' na *be* a next time!' he barked.

'And was there a next time?' we asked the particular tendril of the grapevine that was telling us this story. 'How do they get on now?'

'Oh, he came round completely—eats out of her hand now. Thinks she's wonderful—but then, of course, she is!'

It is always an anxious business when an animal looks like calving in the evening. We don't like to leave our animals totally unattended in this situation, so if the labour has not begun or seems to be in its very early stages at bedtime, we go to bed, but set the alarm to go off at two-hourly intervals during the night, when we take it in turns to go out and see how the situation is developing.

An alarm clock is a rude noise at the best of times, but at two o'clock of a cold frosty morning it is one of the rudest noises I know. Dry-mouthed and heavy-eyed, you drag yourself out of the warm bed, and pull on your trousers and sweater over your night-clothes. The house creaks, eerily, as you tiptoe down the stairs, you repress a shudder as you slip into your cold, clammy boots and outdoor coat. The dogs, piled in slumber before the Aga, raise their heads and look at you blankly, but never offer to come with you. It is moonlight if you are lucky, and you feel very small as you pick your way across the yard under the immensity of the night. A scutter of rats rustles in the straw as you enter the box and switch on the light. One runs over your boot; another disappears, mysteriously, up the wall. Your patient is lying down. Is she in labour, or was it a false alarm? Moving round behind her, you examine the vulva for signs of mucus, blood, or membrane— nothing. Perhaps she is not calving after all? But then you sink your fist into the deep hollows on either side of her tail-head, and feel the hot, tense, engorged udder. Surely she must calve tonight! But she is certainly not doing it at the moment, and you can return to your bed with a clear conscience. The last thing you notice as you switch off the light is that she is not lying with her rear end tight into a corner, or up against a wall. Neighbours have told us lots of stories of cows attempting to calve in such a situation, trying to force the calf out against a wall, and being held up at the critical stage when the calf is half-born. At this stage the calf is compressing his own navel cord, so he is no longer receiving oxygenated blood from his mother, and if he cannot get born and get breathing, it does not take him long to suffocate.

But your cow is lying tidily in the centre of the box, chewing her cud as if she had no thought of calving at all, and so you switch off the light, dash back across the yard, rip off your things again—and with any luck you are back between the sheets again before your side of the bed has had a chance to get any worse than lukewarm. And, the next time the alarm goes, it will be the other one who has to go out, while you, like Othello, merely remark, 'Silence that dreadful bell,' and snuggle down again to sleep.

Cows have many ways of getting acutely ill—you sometimes wonder if they've been reading the veterinary text-books—and one trouble that every dairy farmer meets at some stage in his farming career is milk fever.

'Milk fever' is, as it happens, an exceedingly inappropriate name for this condition, because it is not actually a fever at all. Just the opposite; a cow in its throes has a temperature below normal, and feels icy cold to the touch. Much more descriptive is the proper name, which is hypocalcaemia, meaning a shortage of calcium in the blood.

Nobody knows for sure exactly what makes a cow get milk fever, although there are various theories. It is a metabolic disorder, and occurs either a few days before, or a few days after, calving, when the udder is demanding a lot of calcium from the system for the production of milk. Of course, as everybody knows, milk contains a lot of calcium—that's why it is so good for teeth and bones, calves' as well as ours—and in some cows, the mechanism for providing this peak demand just can't seem to cope, and an acute illness develops.

In practical terms, what happens is this. You go to fetch the cows at milking-time, and it strikes you at once that there is something funny about Clover. (You know what it is when you've seen it once or twice, but we will assume for the sake of the illustration that you are a novice.) She is at the back of the herd instead of the front, her usual place, and she is walking with a strange, stilted gait. Her hind legs are straight, instead of being bent at the hocks, and she has a tendency to stagger. She makes it to the shed, though, and you tie her up, noticing with alarm that her skin is cold, and her eyes fixed in a glassy stare. She ignores the food you put before her, and stands there, straight-legged, swishing her tail, and constantly shifting weight from one one back foot to another, in a regular way that is graphically described as 'paddling'.

Let us hope that by now you are worried enough to send for

153

the vet because if you milk her out, thus stimulating the udder to ask for yet more calcium from her depleted store, to begin the manufacture of the next lot of milk, you will certainly precipitate a crisis. At first she will become excited, and stagger about in a spastic sort of way—then, abruptly, she will go down. Her legs will thrash spasmodically for a few minutes, but eventually she will settle into the classic posture of hypocalcaemia, with head turned right back along her side and eyes still fixed in that hypnotic, glassy stare. Eventually, if no help comes, she will probably die.

But not many people are stupid, or careless, or unlucky enough to lose cows from milk fever these days. For the treatment is so simple. The vet arrives on your yard, drags out of his car-boot the equipment that he always carries—for milk fever is a common occurrence—and runs to your poor cow's side. He puts a small piece of cord tightly round her neck, to raise the vein—then, at the first attempt if he is deft, he inserts a big needle into it. Dark red blood flowing briskly out of the needle shows that he has hit the right spot. Then he uncorks a 500 cc bottle of calcium borogluconate, and, attaching it to a long, rubber tube with a flutter valve, upends it. Clear liquid begins to flow out of the tube, which is then put onto the needle already in the vein, and the cure is under way. You have to be careful not to introduce a bubble of air into the vein—otherwise the operation is pretty straightforward. It takes a few minutes for the stuff to go in—you can adjust the speed of flow by simply raising or lowering the bottle—and as the last drop goes down the tube, the needle is pulled out, and the spot massaged briskly to stop the magic fluid leaking out again. Another bottleful is often put in subcutaneously, on the cow's side, as a further reserve for her to get more slowly.

The action of the intravenous dose is of a speed little short of phenomenal. Within five minutes the cow begins to relax—she blinks her glassy eyes, unwinds her head from its cramped position, and begins to look about her. Then, abruptly, she lurches to her feet. Her hocks are back to their proper angle, her skin is warming up under your very hand, and, putting her head down to the manger, she begins to pull at her hay.

Most farmers keep a few bottles of the calcium solution

154

handy, and administer it subcutaneously, which is usually adequate for a mild or early case. Some will inject it intravenously too, but this is not so easy, and many will not undertake it.

We had many cows with milk fever in our dairying years, but one will always stay particularly in my memory. It was a big black Friesian, called Columbine, and, having started with it during the night, she was in a fairly bad way when we found her in the morning, and we decided she needed an intravenous dose. So we called the vet. It was Sunday, but that could not be helped, and the duty vet, whose name was Phil, duly came out and gave her her bottles. 'I can't stay to see her get up,' he said, trotting briskly back to his car. 'I've got another milk fever to get on to—but she ought to be all right now. Give me another call if she doesn't get up during the morning.' She didn't. Milking came and went, the other cows around her shifted in their stalls and munched their hay; Columbine lay still. From time to time we tried to make her get up, with threats and boot-toe urgings, but though she sometimes surged up as far as her knees, she never made it all the way.

One or two farming neighbours passing, gleaming in their Sunday clothes, noticed the activity in the cowshed and came across to see what was to do. They were full of advice. 'Perhaps she feels the floor too slippery in here, if we could get her out in the yard she'd have a better grip, like.' So we unfastened her neck-chain, and, by concerted heavings, managed to get her facing the other way round in her stall. Then we stimulated her again, and, every time she struggled a bit, she progressed a foot down the passage towards the open door. When she had reached the right level, strong hands swung her round by the tail through 90°, and she somehow scrambled through it. But she did no better outside, and, eventually, the fading light called our neighbours away to begin their own milking.

By this time our yard was beginning to look like something like a cross between a home for geriatric cows and a packing warehouse, for Columbine reclined at her ease against two or three bales of straw, artfully pushed up to save her from rolling over; and on her back, a motley collection of sacks, tied on with binder-twine, protected her from the chilly drizzle that

155

had begun to fall. It was clear to us that she wasn't going to get up that evening under her own steam, and equally clear that she couldn't stay out all night. So, reluctantly, we telephoned Phil again.

He didn't sound too put out. 'All right, I'll be with you in a quarter of an hour,' he said. 'Leave the yard gate open for me.'

People were beginning to go to evening chapel by now, and several sets of headlights swept, blazing, past our lane-end. We waited on the yard, beside our cow, in the gathering gloom. Columbine lay, impassive. How would he manage her?

And then we knew. The next car along the road turned in at the gate, instead of passing up the lane—and with lights blazing and a great blare of the horn, accelerated straight up the yard towards the prostrate cow! I have never seen an animal move so fast in all my life. Thunderstruck, galvanised, she leapt to her feet, scattering sacks and bales in every direction, and rushed in through the cowshed door to the peace and security of her own stall. Phil reversed round, and wound down his window. 'We've made great strides in veterinary science these last few years,' he remarked. 'We don't even have to get out of the car to treat 'em now! Goodnight!'

Another cow I remember was a slightly unfortunate case of milk fever, because she needed a bottle subcutaneously, and we couldn't find our 'flutter valve', the rubber thing that dribbles the stuff out of the bottle. We had to inject the stuff instead —and the only syringe available was a tiny one of ten cc's! So Desmond inserted one needle into her side, and another into the bottle and the syringe itself was transferred from one to the other—filling from the bottle, emptying into the cow—fifty times! She got rather restive before it was over, but it did do the trick for her, albeit at the cost of some discomfort.

Some people use the term 'milk fever' very strangely indeed, like one old man, who looked over the cowshed door one day at one of our cows that was in bed with a cold, so to speak. She was lying rather sadly in her stall, with a little dribble of mucus coming from her nose, and the ancient wasted no time in offering us his diagnosis. 'Do you know what is the matter with that cow? Milk fever, yes, indeed. Now all the milk that is in

156

her has run into her head—see the way she is holding her head down, now—and until it goes from there she won't be well. Look, there is some milk coming out of her nose now!' It is hard to credit that this was offered as a serious theory, but it was. He did not, however, advise us about treatment.

IV

As the years have gone by, we have gradually made ourselves some kind of a place in the community, a fact which is to both of us, cut off as we are from our own native roots, a source of much pleasure and satisfaction. People know us now—our strengths and our limitations—the fact that we never seem to be very tidy, for instance, but that we are glad to contribute to the local charities—they can pretty well guess how we will react in any given situation.

But it was not always so. When we first came to Penllwyn-plan, we represented something of an enigma, and some of our behaviour was seen as wildly eccentric; a point of view that was partly fostered by an interview that Matthew had with a visiting representative shortly after our arrival.

Not that Matthew normally answered the door; he was only just three. But it so happened that both Desmond and I had simultaneously been obliged to attend to the calls of nature, and as we had two lavatories, we had each betaken ourselves to one of them—me upstairs, and Desmond in the outside one, at the end of a short garden path. Here enthroned, he could easily hear what went on as a rep. drew up on the yard, got out of his car, walked up the path, and knocked on the door. Matthew, realising that he was temporarily in charge of the business, answered it, and the following conversation took place.

Rep. (ingratiatingly) 'Helloa! Where's Mammy, then?'

Matthew (in his clear, beautifully enunciated voice) 'Mummy's upstairs doing biggy.'

(A stunned pause.)

Rep. 'Oah! Where's Daddi, then?'

Matthew. 'Daddy's outside, doing biggy.'

(Another dead pause, the rep. clearly totally nonplussed.

Then Matthew, a child with well-developed social instincts, clearly feeling that the ball was in his court this time, remarked:

'It *is* a lovely day, isn't it?'

And when Desmond took pity on the poor man and emerged from his confinement he found that Matthew had removed his short trousers and was conducting this conversation urinating discreetly into the drain beside the step. Poor rep.! He must have thought he'd strayed into a camp of excretion maniacs.

I don't know whether this story got around, or whether our countrymen have a reputation, but a rather quaint thing was said to us soon afterwards, in a builder's merchant, in Carmarthen. We had gone in to get a new rubber joint for our upstairs lavatory, because the joint where the flush comes into the pan had perished, and was leaking. We had already replaced it once in our short tenancy of the farm, and here it was, leaking again, a fact which we commented on, rather plaintively, to the elderly man in the shop. He looked at us sharply over the tops of his half-glasses, summing us up, his lips closed, like a trap. Then he shot a question.

'English, are you?' We nodded.

'You need a heavy duty one!'

What a national reputation! But he was right—we did.

Moving from our suburban situation made a great difference to the children's way of life, for the tightly organised playgroups and baby-sitting rotas of the suburbs simply didn't exist here, and nor did all the little frilly birthday parties and things. In exchange, they got a much freer range to play in, and much more scope for creative mess-making, and the company of large numbers of animals, including a succession of puppies and kittens, still happily continuing.

But that wasn't all they got. They also picked up language which was never heard in the chaste avenues of Welwyn (though one little boy in the play-group did tell me I was a wicked bugger over some minor point of discipline) and we struggled constantly to teach them the double standard—with very partial success. Not that they set out to shock. I can quite see that if you hear one word used for something by virtually everybody, you think that is the word for it, and that is all there is to it. But in some circles they were considered a trifle coarse.

My aunt—their great-aunt—was taking them back in her car for a holiday in London once, when they were very small. As they drove along they passed a mare in a field that was preparing to urinate, and cramping itself into the strained, gothic attitude that mares adopt for the process. 'What's that horse doing, Aunty Mary?' asked Rachel. 'Oh, it's just going to wee-wee, or whatever you call it,' said Aunty Mary. Matthew turned round, politely explanatory. 'Actually, we call it pissing,' he said.

Not that it was only the children who said funny things. A neighbour once made a very quotable, and indeed much-quoted remark. We had been raising fifty cockerels for an order, and had been let down at the last minute. So we plucked and dressed the cockerels, put them, each in his polythene bag, in the deep freeze, and looked around for a buyer. We had one man in mind, whose brother was a butcher, and who occasionally came to the farm to buy calves or barren cows from us. The next time he visited us, we mentioned the chicken, and he said that he thought his brother might be interested in them if we could agree on a price. 'But let's finish with the outside business first, is it?' he said. So we all repaired to the covered yard and talked about the cow we wanted him to buy, he trying to beat our price down, we sticking a bit. We came to a compromise in the end, and went into the house to talk about the chickens. 'Get 'em out on the table—let's have a look at them,' he said, so we piled them up, all fifty, frozen stiffly in their polythene shrouds, in a big pyramid on the table. We were standing round them, still in our outdoor clothes, with gloves on—our buyer, indeed, wearing a fur hat, for it was a black-frost day—when a neighbour knocked on the door and walked into the kitchen. She looked at us blankly, and said, 'Can I have a couple of dozen eggs please?' then, as I accompanied her across to the egg room to get them, she added, memorably, 'I am sorry to have interrupted you in the middle of your dinner!' She must have thought we ate in the manner of sled dogs, who are flung a ration of frozen meat which they bolt, incontinently. Even so, fifty between three of us would surely have meant second helpings.

We find plenty to laugh at, and of course not by any means

all of it is unintentional humour. Charlie, our neighbour in the market, an ex-Metropolitan mounted policeman, of whom I have written in my first book, had a bon mot the other day. He was talking to Desmond when a woman customer came up, and rallied the pair of them with, 'Chattering again, is it? I thought it was the women who were supposed to be the talkers!' Charlie turned to her, politely. 'As a matter of fact,' he said, 'that is a theory to which I have never subscribed personally. I've met some very dumb women in my time!'

It is in the market, of course, where we go every Wednesday and Saturday, to sell our eggs, that we have the best chance of hearing the lively anecdotes with which Welsh country life is spiced. Most Welshmen are good raconteurs, and only need the slightest encouragement to embark on a story. If you can get a couple of them telling contrapuntally, so to speak, you are right for a couple of hours' entertainment, for they egg each other on, in emulation, the stories getting taller and taller, as time goes by.

At one such session recently, we were treated to the story of the Orphan and the Postman. This took place, it appears, up in the hill country of North Wales, where the man who was telling us the story had an old aunty, with whom he used to spend his holidays. Now this aunty had a neighbour who was a great big man called Gruffydd, strong as an ox, and savage as a wolf, a hard man in every way, and one not lightly to be crossed. Everyone was careful not to offend him, and he was as bad-tempered and awkward to his own wife and children as to anybody else. There was, indeed, only one soft spot in his heart, and this was reserved for his nephew. This boy, the only child of the big farmer's only sister, was orphaned at an early age, and came to live with Griff and his family. And, oddly enough, although he was in general a timid, shrinking sort of lad, the boy never showed any fear of Griff, but, rather, turned to him for help in every difficulty. The bond between them was strong, and remained so, even when the boy grew up, and, in due course, fell in love with a local girl, and became engaged to be married. Griff it was who helped him find a cottage in the neighbourhood to rent, and Griff who helped him decorate it, ready for the bride, and furnish it with the bare necessities that were all that he could, at first, afford.

160

The wedding day came, and the young couple settled down to their new life. The nephew worked hard and lived frugally, happily putting all he could save into the beautifying of his little home—more poignantly dear to him, perhaps in that, as an orphan, he had never really had a place of his very own before. His charming wife kept herself and the house pretty and neat, and for a year or so, all went as merry as a marriage bell. But a serpent lurked in this Eden in the form of a young and handsome postman and, at this juncture, he raised his head. At first with disbelief, then with anxiety, then with a kind of sick hurt, the nephew saw which way the wind was blowing. Certainly, it was a long walk from the road to the cottage—it was kind of his wife to make the postman a cup of tea when the weather was cold. But need she do it every day? And need she sit down at the table to have one with him leaning towards him like that, hanging on his every word, laughing at his jokes, while her own husband sat by, sullen and neglected? Was his new-found bliss to be so soon destroyed? What could he do? In his perplexity, he turned to his uncle—the old friend, who had helped him so often before, and laid the whole situation open to him, with all its fearful implications. What did Griff think he should do?

Griff, of course was furious. His eyes flashed, and he thumped his fist on the table, before jumping up to stride up and down the room in his rage.

'Hell! Hell! she fancies him, does she? You're not good enough, is it?' he shouted. His nephew nodded, despondently.

'Castrating! That's what he needs!' roared Griff. 'Should have put a rubber ring on him at birth! I'd take the pincers to him for two pins! That's what a man like that needs.'

But forcible castration being obviously out of the question, Griff simmered down, and said he would think about the situation, and tell the boy in a day or two what he should do. The castration motif lingered in his mind, however, and, next morning at breakfast, he was suddenly struck by a bright idea. He hastened off to his vet.

'You know when you want to castrate a cockerel,' he started. 'Those little white pills, you know!'

'Oh, the stilboestrol caponising pellets that you implant in the neck,' replied the vet, all unsuspecting. 'Yes, I've got some —how many do you want to do?'

'About fifty, I reckon!' and Griff hurried away with his booty, mentally rubbing his hands. 'Gets a cup of tea every day, does he, the bobby-dazzler!' he muttered to himself. 'Wonder if he takes sugar?'

'And *did* he manage to caponise the postman?' we asked breathlessly.

'Well, *no*, he didn't, in the end, but just luck it was. He tried a few experiments at home with the crushed tablets in tea, but it didn't work at all. It all floated up to the top—anyone would've noticed it. So then he began to try putting it in fruit cake, and after a couple of goes he got that quite good. But then, just when he had it ready, the postman got promoted, and moved away. And that was the end of that.'

'What happened to the nephew and his wife?' we enquired, wanting to get all the loose ends of the story tied up.

'Oh, she was poody for a bit, but she settled down, and then about a year later she got a baby. She didn't have any time for postmen and things after that.'

V

I often wonder if the great joy that farming was to me when I was a child had something to do with the fact that I was playing at it rather than working at it. Now, after nearly fourteen years of earning our living by farming and by nothing else, Desmond and I must surely qualify as 'real' farmers, although our attitudes will always be coloured by our urban origins. So perhaps it is reasonable, if I allow myself to count as a 'real' farmer, to ask the question again; is farming still fun, or has familiarity and financial stress knocked the gilt off the gingerbread?

It is difficult to give an unconditional answer to that question. I would not want to be anything but a farmer, but there is no denying that the work which is most enjoyable is not that which is commercially the most successful. I still find, in farming, the kernel of what I hoped, as a child, I might find in it;

but with every new farming technique that is introduced, a bit of the old magic departs, and there is no doubt in my mind that a viable commercial farm of today is a much less 'farmy' place than it would have been, say, forty years ago.

Take my own day's work as an illustration—a day, for example, in January 1977, with the farm stocked with about 3,000 laying hens in batteries, and a small herd of twenty-three Welsh Black cows, suckling their own calves.

Although we get up at 7.30 we are seldom out of the house before nine o'clock these days, except on market days. By then, it will be light, and while Desmond goes off to open up the henshed and feed the birds, my first job is to feed the cattle.

Our cattle this year are on a regimen of straw and rolled oats in the mornings, and hay in the evenings, when they are shut up for the night. During the daylight hours they are free to roam the fields at will, and seem to find something to graze most of the time. On frosty days, I put the straw out for them in the field, spreading it out well, so that even the timid ones get a chance to eat their share. I love a bright, frosty morning; I still take delight in the crunch of my foot through the ice of a puddle, the star-shaped shatter as I plod, bale on my back, over the deeply hoof-packed mud to the drier, greener bit of the field further away from the yard. This is the field that the oats were grown on last summer, so it doesn't matter that the cattle mess it up with their feet. A 'sacrifice field' is what such a piece of land is called; in spring, when the weather is dry enough, it will be ploughed and re-seeded for a new pasture.

When I have got past the worst of the frozen craters, and no longer have to pick my way so carefully, I raise my head and enjoy the scene around me. The village, still white with frost, nestles in the valley below, a charming jumble of trees and buildings. The squat grey church on its rocky bluff looks over the rounded tops of its great blackish-green yew trees; the rosy brick of the church hall and the ochre walls of the pub warmly reflect the brilliant sunlight which sparkles off the little river looping away through its flat meadows. Smoke from a dozen chimneys rises straight into the air, and distant sounds—a dog barking, metallic hammerings from the forge, a milk lorry changing down to breast the Trelech hill—come, muted, through the clean air. And, all around, the green fields in gracious, rounded hills, furred with wooded valleys and pranked with little streams.

Near at hand, there is plenty of life. Meadow-pipits with streaky plumage and fragile pink legs, flit from tussock to tussock ahead of me. A wren, stump-tailed, zooms rapidly from a fallen tree-stump to a clump of brambles in the ditch. A bevy of sparrows is already quarrelling, vociferously, on the bale I dumped on my last trip; and a buzzard, sunning himself close by in the top branches of a young ash tree, keeps up a continuous commentary of rather petulant mewing.

Five cats accompany me to and fro as I fetch the four bales of straw from the Dutch barn and carry them, one by one, down the field. I walk a good deal faster than they do, so they describe a sort of miniature of my journey, including only its middle section. They never get as far up the field as the yard before they meet me coming back with the next bale, and then they turn and follow me, only to be left behind again, and to meet me coming back for my next trip. When all four bales are out I wait for them, though, and they all hasten up to take part, each in its own way, in the spreading of the straw.

Miss Moppet is the senior cat, and she jumps on to each golden bale as I come up to it. She has to be picked up and stroked for a moment, and then gently placed on the ground before I can remove the bale-strings and separate the straw into 'biscuits' for the cows. Beaver, who is younger, leaps onto my back at every opportunity, and clings adventurously with blazing eyes. Luckily for me, I am wearing a thick padded anorak. Rafiq, the black kitten, rises on his back legs to shadow-box the neck-string of my anorak every time I bend down. Ribby and Peabody, two irresponsible stripy youngsters, roll each other over in mock combat, or make futile pounces at the passing shadows of two ravens who fly past, stunting and side-slipping, two hundred feet over our heads.

With the straw spread, we return to the yard to put out the oats. This is the first year that we have grown grain, and we were lucky to get a good yield considering the frightful drought that blasted so many corn crops in 1976. Luckily our oats were drilled on March 1, and were just far enough on to make decent-sized plants before the drought really struck. From our six-acre field we harvested 8½ tons of grain and 460 bales of good bright straw—not record-breaking yields, to be sure, but not shameful either, in such a difficult year.

I should have liked to see great flaring breadths of scarlet poppies in our corn, in defiance of all the laws of good farming, but my efforts in that direction were not crowned with a very striking success. I scattered some seed along one edge of the field, but in the drought it never germinated; and the couple of dozen plants that I transplanted into the standing corn remained pitifully small and stunted. I did get a poppy or two—a spark rather than a blaze—but you had to know just where to look, and then you had to go down on your knees and part the corn, and pull the chickweed and stuff to one side ... I didn't show anyone my corn poppies. I felt it was all too silly.

The oats, ready rolled, are exceedingly pleasing and satisfactory things to have. We have not many troughs to feed them in, so the bulk of them are just tipped out onto the edges of the yard, where the concrete is licked spotlessly clean by the cows every day. The cows can see the fluffy crushed grain being put out, and a chorus of impatient moos rends the air. I unlatch the gate and skip out of the way, and out they come with a rush. Like bargain-hunters at a sale, they advance at a shuffling trot, and soon every head is down in a concentrated silence of ingestion.

By now Desmond has finished feeding the birds, and together we address ourselves to cleaning out the building where the cattle have spent the night. I keep writing about the pleasure of shovelling up muck—people will begin to think I am a coprophiliac—but it is a pleasure, particularly on a lovely brisk day when there isn't too much of it, and the powerful, rhythmic movements of shovelling bring a glow of well-being without exhausting you.

So far so good; my day's work up till about 10.30 has been idyllic, a series of pleasures of which I never tire. But now comes the rub. The cattle alone do not produce anything like enough for us to live on, and work with the battery hens who provide our main income is hardly like farming at all. For the next hour or so I must collect eggs, in the warm, frowsty, dimly-lit henshed, totally divorced from the sun and the sky and the wind, and the views of distant scenery or passing birds and beasts. I am not complaining about my lot—but the intensification of farming, however much it has improved its efficiency, has certainly taken a lot of the pleasure out of it. The only satisfaction you can get from egg collecting and grading is the ordinary bread-and-butter satisfaction of getting through a set quantity of work—a satisfaction which is no different in a farmyard or in a factory. For sheer uplift, looking after caged hens in no way compares with working around the cattle.

Egg work—collecting, grading, boxing—takes up all the middle of the day. In the afternoons we sometimes dress poultry for the table, another unpopular job—and then the seven bales of hay for the cattle must be put out in their covered yard, and they themselves fetched in, counted, and shut up before dark.

My work about the farm is fairly circumscribed. I have the housework and cooking to do, and as I also have the ultimate brown thumb in all matters concerning machinery, I am as far as possible insulated from it, for everyone's sake. Desmond does the tractor work and all the egg deliveries and all sorts of jobs like getting the oats crushed. He also organises anything like contractors, and keeps the books of the farm business. But the thing I am most grateful of all to him for shouldering is that, when machines go wrong, it is he who puts them right.

And machines do go wrong. One of the most boring things about mechanisation is that you become dependent on it, and then when, inevitably, something goes wrong with it, you are in trouble. You circumvent the trouble—you have to—but it means that the work is constantly being made harassing instead of smooth.

In this, I am fully aware that I write as a woman. The men seem to take an absolute delight in machinery, in buying it, using it, mending it, selling it—I remember one neighbour's dark eyes positively sparkling with zest as he told us about his new big tractor, and how he intended to take full advantage of its strength, and push it to the very limits of its performance in order to get his silage cut quickly that year. 'You'll hear her really *grunting* when we get on that bit of a slope with a load behind her! Black smoke'll be *pourin'* out of her!' 'As long as you give her plenty of cocoa!' replied another neighbour, and they both laughed gleefully at the prospect.

Most of the field work of the farm is tractor work now, even hedge cutting, for long the last refuge of the skilled hand. In an effort to save our tractor, we get contractors in to do quite a lot of the seasonal field jobs, like the odd bit of ploughing, or cutting and baling the hay. Not that our tractor seems in any way appreciative; it still breaks down from time to time, leaving us with the weekly problem of getting the muck away from the henshed.

Carrying hay is the one operation that still calls for hand labour in the fields, and in 1976 its laboriousness was intensified by the frightful heat in which one had to work. As it turned out, we could have safely brought it into the barn at the rate of about fifty bales a day, but of course we had no means of knowing how long the hot weather would last, and we all pushed on as briskly as we knew how. We only had a thousand bales to carry, but there was no help to be had, so we had to carry them all between the two of us, on our ridiculous little trailer that will only take a load of about forty bales. I seem to have a totally inadequate cooling system, and I really began to wonder if I would explode with overheating. 'Mummy! you *are red!*' the children kept saying with horrified admiration— but there was no relief anywhere. If you decided to sink down for a few minutes' rest and sought the few tiny patches of shade under the hedges you found that they were sheltered even from the tiny, tired wind that was blowing, and sitting down on the parched earth there made you hotter than ever. Only the flies had energy; they buzzed, maddeningly, in burnished battalions, all around you or walked over your sweating face with inexplicably cool feet.

Feeling, by about two o'clock on the first day, that we were courting physical collapse, we left the field, and instead set our alarm for four o'clock the following morning. What a difference that made! There was not much dew, it is true—everything was too dry for dew to form, and the brown, cracked earth still felt warm to the hand—but the air was cool, the birds were singing, and swathes of scent from the dog roses and honey-suckles in the hedge alternated with the overall sweetness of

167

the hay as we bumped and jolted down the field to pick up our first load.

Many people we knew did make themselves quite ill with heat-exhaustion—an interesting comment on the independent man's sternness towards his own physical weakness. Some farmers took to working at night, which was quite a sensible solution. It was hard, though, on those whose bedroom windows were near the fields in which the tractors roared and swung their brilliant headlights around all through the small hours. But hay is king in a country district, and it would be considered very improper to complain.

In the event, the drought continued for many weeks after the haymaking, and our corn ripened and was combined in a flurry of dust. We were able to bale and carry the straw on the very next day, and the stubble lay, palely gleaming, dry as a desert beneath the pitiless sun. I used to walk across it every day on my way to fill the cows' water trough, and I was intrigued to see evidence of shallow scratchings-up all over the field. Perhaps they were field-mouse burrows excavated by foxes. Neither the dogs nor the cats, who always came with me, took any interest in them, so if they had been mouse-holes, the smell must have quickly dissipated.

On the day before the rain came, I walked down over the stubble as usual. There was nothing to indicate that our great trial was almost at an end. The sky was pale blue, the sun brassy as ever. The fields rolled, brown and sere, to the horizon, between hedges already beginning to drop their wilting leaves. But, halfway down the field, I stopped. Something was different! I listened carefully. Yes, that was it! All around me, the cut stubble was exploding in a fusillade of merry little reports—crack-crack-crack, over the whole field, like tiny distant rifle-fire. There was nothing to see, but presumably a change of humidity in the air was somehow setting off these miniature crackers in the parched stems of the stubble. It was like walking over a big bowl of rice crispies.

In the day-to-day work of the farm, there are still these opportunities for the aspects of farming that seem to me to give it its essential quality. Erecting a fence, going down to the spring from which the hens' water is pumped, to check that it has not got choked with dead leaves, counting the cattle in the fields every day in summer—these are all jobs which take you out of doors, among the birds and flowers and weather-signs. The simple pleasure is still there.

But nobody could say the same about the other pleasure one might have expected to get from farming—the pleasure of a good business building up its resources, of land farmed tightly to its utmost capacity, of continuity in the association of one family with one farm, which makes it sensible to build for the future. Who bothers to plant an oak wood now, since the Socialist credo of envy and spoliation has breathed its blight over the farming industry? It pays you neither to work hard for immediate income, which will instantly be whipped away from you in the form of income tax, nor to lay up for your children's benefit, for capital transfer tax will ensure that no farm of any size can be handed on as a working unit, and once that principle is accepted, who can say how long it will be before the smaller farms too are considered too privilege-conferring to be handed on? The situation is summed up in a verse from *The Rubá 'iyát of E. Cragoe*, which says:

> 'Alike to those who for today prepare,
> And those who after a tomorrow stare,
> A muezzin from the House of Transport cries
> "Fools! Your reward is neither here nor there!"'

I appreciate that it is not easy to run a modern industrial society, and we who live in it are lucky that the government can draw on the advice of many wise men who have made a lifetime study of economics. But, looking at today's situation with a non-economist's eye, it seems both silly and lamentable that one and a half million people should stand about unemployed, while the cars, television sets, typewriters, cameras and so on that they are trained to make are imported from other countries and paid for by borrowed money, against which we pledge— what? A further fatuity is lent to the situation by the fact that the farmers of this country have their prices so rigged that they too cannot afford to employ this vast pool of labour, and many of our rich acres remain grossly under-utilised so that we have to compound our indebtedness by importing the food we could perfectly well grow ourselves. That people who have made a special study of economics should lead us into such a Gilbertian situation leads me to only one conclusion—*The Economists Have Got No Clothes On!*

Having been thinking this for some time, I was fascinated to read, in Cobbett's *Rural Rides*, one of my 1976 Christmas presents, the following passage:

'From the Bourne we proceeded onto Wrecklesham, at the end of which we crossed what is called the river Wey. Here we found a parcel of labourers at parish-work. Amongst them was an old playmate of mine. The account they gave of their situation was very dismal. The harvest was over early. The hop-picking is now over; and now they are employed by the parish; that is to say, not absolutely digging holes one day and filling them up the next; but at the expense of half-ruined farmers and tradesmen and landlords, to break stones into very small pieces to make nice smooth roads lest the jostling, in going along them, should create bile in the stomachs of the overfed tax-eaters. I call upon mankind to witness this scene; and to say, whether the like of this was heard of before. It is a state of things where all is out of order; where self-preservation, that great law of nature, seems to be set at defiance for here are farmers *unable* to pay men for working for them, and yet compelled to pay them for working in doing that which is really no use to any human being. There lie the hop-poles unstripped. You see a hundred things in the neighbouring fields that want doing. The fences are not nearly what they ought to be. The very meadows, to our right and our left in crossing this little valley, would occupy these men advantageously until the setting in of the frost; and here are they, not, as I said before, actually digging holes one day and filling them up the next; but, to all intents and purposes, as uselessly employed.'

That was written in 1822, and quite evidently the economists who devised the ridiculous Speenhamland system of outdoor relief had no clothes on either. That means that they have been running around naked for at least 150 years; is it too much to hope that they will eventually die of exposure, leaving the field open to people who act more on the principle of common sense?

It is a curious freak of our history that has led people to feel that people who produce necessities somehow *ought* to be less well remunerated than people who produce luxuries. Because we once had an empire from which, either by the exploitation of slaves or the rape of natural resources like the prairies, cheap food could be sent home to the mother-country, we tend to down-grade food in our scheme of things; and it seems only right and natural to most people that a man who spends forty hours a week in a car factory screwing up nuts with an automatic machine should be paid twice as much as a skilled herdsman in sole charge of a herd of high-yielding pedigree Friesians. I do not think it is right and natural; I think it is wrong and silly. Surely food is of all our needs the most basic? And surely nobody could deny that the farm labourer's job, with all its skills, is both harder and more difficult than the assembly line worker's? And yet the conventions demand that food should be cheap, cars dear.

But of course although the economic and political aspects of farming are at present unsatisfactory, and although the dreadful, noisy, accident-prone machine has encroached on our quiet, farming is still farming. We still live deep in the country; we still concern ourselves daily with animals and crops, weather and seasons, harvesting and renewal; we can still enjoy all the peripheral bounty of our way of life, like making elderflower wine or crab-apple jelly from our own wild hedgerows. If we look at our own day-by-day lives, we find that much of what we thought we were nostalgic for is still there, only superficially altered by our growing up and the dubious progress of our civilisation.

We still have the pleasure and the privilege of walking about our own acres, monarchs of all we survey, and of planning how we shall spend what resources we have, in work or in pleasure. Shall we grow oats in Cae Isaf this year? Or would it be better to take a crop of barley off Cae Gwair before reseeding it? Would it be a good idea to plant a small copse in that out-of-the-way corner of the dip? And could a bulldozer possibly get down that steep slope, to scrape a frog-pond in that rushy bit where the stream comes out from under the hill?

The warm sun coaxes out the amber leaves of the great oaks standing, immemorial, around you. It is time to go back to the farmhouse and get on with that order for six oven-ready chickens for tomorrow's market. But, for a moment, you linger. A woodpigeon, high overhead, coos vehemently its endless suggestion, 'Take *two* cows, Taffy, *do*', and down by the stream a green woodpecker's maniacal laugh echoes through the hazels. Nearby, the current season's crop of calves graze busily, little black tails flicking to keep the flies at bay. It is all very peaceful.

Yes, it is still worth while being a farmer.